D1276701

CUTTING
PAPERWORK
IN THE
CORPORATE CULTURE

CUTTING PAPERWORK IN THE CORPORATE CULTURE

Dianna Booher

Facts On File Publications
New York, New York • Oxford, England

CUTTING PAPERWORK IN THE CORPORATE CULTURE

Library of Congress Cataloging-in-Publication Data

Booher, Dianna Daniels.

  Cutting paperwork in the corporate culture.

  Bibliography: p.
  Includes index.
  1. Paperwork (Office practice)—Management. I. Title.
HF5547.15.B66 1986   651.7   85-31204
ISBN 0-8160-1343-8

Printed in the United States of America
10 9 8 7 6 5 4 3 2 1

Composition by Facts On File/Circle Graphics

CONTENTS

10. How to Get the Most from Your Secretarial Support Staff

"Uh, ... ah, ... I guess my secretary didn't catch that. I'll have

11. Writing Training

INTRODUCTION

I've written this book at the risk of writing myself out of a livelihood. As a consultant, I get paid to teach people to write better memos, letters, reports, proposals. So why am I now saying to the corporate world, "Stop putting it in writing"?

Let me explain: When I go into an organization, I feel much like the family doctor who sees a dangerously ill uncle, prescribes medication, and then doesn't know whom to tell to make sure the uncle follows the advice and takes the medicine.

I get to read the company's internal mail and find out, in effect, where the organization hurts, but there is rarely anybody totally responsible for seeing that the organization as a whole becomes aware of its paper disease.

Consider this book "written notice," complete with prescription.

COSTS OF PAPERWORK

Productivity Costs

Blue-collar productivity has increased 90 percent during the last two decades, while white-collar productivity has increased only 4 percent.

Why? The following answers surface from various sources: White-collar workers push more and more paper and take less and less action. White-collar workers do not have a clear grasp of the really necessary administrative functions. They do not manage people well in that they do not solicit their workers' suggestions on ways to do their jobs better;

1

they do not give their staff adequate directions for tasks; and they do not use available technology for gathering and communicating information efficiently.

Studies of American business indicate that 50 to 70 percent of all working hours are spent on paperwork. That paperwork includes preparing, reading, recording, interpreting, filing, and maintaining information.

And we are losing the war against this paperwork disease. The clerical force, now the largest segment of the white-collar workforce in the United States, accounts for 37 percent of that group, including professional and technical workers, managers and administrators, and salespeople. From my general impressions over the last six years of working with thousands of white-collar workers and with a formal survey of 657 employees in 14 companies from seven different industries, I find that paperwork consumes the following percentage of employee time. (Although respondents on the surveys were *not* scientifically selected, the results are fairly representative of organizations as a whole. The fact that the surveys were conducted in writing workshops does not necessarily mean that only those who tend to do the most writing in the organization responded. In fact, 33 percent of the respondents estimated that they spend 10 percent or less of their time writing. Survey responses can be broken down as follows: senior managers, 20 percent; middle managers, 24 percent; professionals, 36 percent, clerical, 20 percent.)

Estimated time spent in both writing and reading job-related materials:

- Senior managers   46%
- Middle managers   45%
- Professionals with no
  supervisory responsibilities   40%
- Clerical support staff   51%

For an estimate of what your company spends on paperwork each year, multiply your payroll in each group by the above percentages. In some organizations, such as research firms, banks, insurance companies, and brokerage houses, the percentage of time spent on paperwork is even greater than these averages.

A 1985 study done by Accountemps through an independent research organization found that poor management is directly responsible for poor productivity 55 percent of the time. The study, reported in *Training & Development Journal* (July 1985), was based on interviews with vice presidents and personnel directors of 100 of America's 1,000 largest companies. The study further pinpointed the management failures as, for example, lack of adequate supervision; failure to provide motivation, incentive, and direction; and insufficient or poorly planned communications.

A 1982 Booz, Allen, & Hamilton study of 300 knowledge workers found that they spend less than half of their work time on activities directly related to their functions. The same study reports that professionals spend an average of 21 percent of their time in document preparation and review, and only 8 percent on analysis.

Knowledge workers can't give or gain "knowledge" because they're too bogged down in paper.

Records Handling/Retention/Retrieval Costs

According to various form designers and records management experts and governmental and private-industry research studies:

- Sixty percent of all clerical work is spent on checking, filing, and retrieving information; that leaves only 40 percent of clerical time for more important tasks such as data processing and communication.
- Americans create 30 billion original documents annually.
- Paperwork costs over $100 billion annually in the U.S.
- We write hundreds of letters, memos, and reports that are completely meaningless.
- Seventy-five to 85 percent of documents that we retain we never again refer to.
- Sixty-five cents of every dollar spent on record-keeping is wasted on unnecessary files and duplicate copies.
- We misfile 3 percent of all documents we need.
- For every dollar spent on printing forms, we spend $20-80 to process them, copy and distribute them, store them, and destroy them.
- We spend $25,000 to print and process the forms in a four-drawer file cabinet of 18,000 pages.
- We spend $2,160 annually to maintain an active four-drawer file of 18,000 pages.
- We maintain 18,000 pages (or a four-drawer file cabinet) for *each* white-collar employee, and this file size increases 4,000 pages per year for each employee.

- The average company spends $29,000 annually to maintain its files.

But these productivity and records-retention figures don't give nearly the whole picture of paperwork costs. Consider the following.

Sales and Service to Customers

Consider the intangible costs such as loss of potential sales because customers and clients

- refuse to read lengthy boilerplate proposals or sales letters
- distrust your product or service because of inaccurate information or incomprehensible correspondence (Yes, buyers notice poor communication. A district manager of a utility company recently told me that he had received an ad from one of the Fortune 500 companies with six errors. He circled the errors and sent it back to the company, explaining why he wasn't buying their equipment.)
- get angry because you can't find their records and handle them correctly
- get tired of the paperwork and delays required to deal with you

Employee Morale

Another cost of paperwork difficult to measure, but nevertheless important to consider, is employee morale. Most employees view paperwork as the drudge part of their jobs. Additionally, paperwork stifles intrapreneurial creativity. To encourage new ideas, managers have to free their people to work through promising ideas without the harassment of bureaucratic paperwork and delay.

WHERE DID WE CONTRACT THE PAPER DISEASE?

Much is "hereditary." We are born with the idea that important events and agreements are recorded on paper—births, deaths, grades, taxes, wills, marriage licenses, vehicle registrations, voter registrations, draft cards, Social Security numbers, mortgages, insurance policies, certificates of deposit, stock certificates. Paper has been with us to record important events for centuries. In fact, many of us grew up with the idea that words were magical—like Abbra-ca-dabra. Some would-be smooth-talkers still think there is magic in writing, magic that transforms the ordinary to the official.

Some people are exposed to the paper disease in schools. Teachers may have graded on effort: If students never learned the battle dates of the Civil War but could sketch the layout of the Appomattox Courthouse, they often got extra credit for the extra paperwork. So, in the business world, if employees generate a lot of paperwork, they sometimes get credit even if they haven't met company objectives.

Just as paperwork on a school desk was a sign to the teacher that the students were busy, so also many employees keep lots of paper around to show others how busy they are. In fact, if you ever have time to wander the halls in your office building and you notice a desk with no paperwork on it, what's your immediate reaction? Probably that it's a vacant office—that somebody's been moved. Paper symbolizes work to many people.

Finally, school taught us that more is better. Do you remember all those assignments by length? "I want a 500-word essay on sibling rivalry"—a parallel to assignments by length in the business world? The more money people want to spend or the more attention they want to get for an idea, the longer the report they write. Engineers, particularly, are trained to get in every possible detail; detail, to them, means thoroughness and protection if things don't go well with their project.

In addition to "heredity" and educational training, some people succumb to the paper disease through personality disorders:

- paranoia about being blamed for errors
- distrust of anyone who doesn't "put it in writing"
- insecurities about how they're perceived in the company
- constant need for reassurance that "they're on the right track"
- inability to delegate without constant "report backs"
- phobias about computers and information not in hard copy
- lack of confidence to be articulate face to face
- the thrill of checking records and finding minuscule mistakes to validate self-worth
- frustration created by those who've missed their calling as novelists

The psychological causes for paperwork are endless.

CAN THE DISEASE BE CURED OR CONTROLLED?

Have you ever worked for a small, newly established company? Do you remember when three or four staff members met in the hall for a quick stand-up meeting, discussed a problem, and somebody took immediate action to solve it? Small organizations make great headway on their competition by doing just that—talking instead of writing.

This is not to say that we can live in a paperless corporate society. As any organization grows, it will find some paperwork necessary, especially that imposed by the government. But some companies don't stop at this low-grade fever; they let paper run rampant until it has become an organization-wide epidemic that demands major surgery.

Can this paperwork disease really be controlled or cured? Yes. Let me cite two examples: IBM Brazil and the Marks and Spencer company.

Derek Rayner, writing in the *Harvard Business Review*, reports the success of Marks and Spencer, a clothing and housewares retailer in England and Wales, back in the late 1950s. They eliminated 26 million forms used annually and gradually reduced their staff from 27,000 to 20,000. Their goal was not only to save money on paperwork but also to use their resources more effectively. They were successful; they doubled their sales between 1963 and 1972.

How did they do it? They entitled their campaign "Good Housekeeping." They had their top management get out and wander around to spot the unnecessary paperwork. Why did top management do the wandering? Because no one would argue about the value of a certain report when top management considered it unnecessary and costly.

In addition to needless reports, these top executives at Marks and Spencer found an ignorance of how much paperwork processing really costs. Their employees had little concept of how each piece of paper they originated created a chain of related paperwork. Their staffs were spending excessive time in verifying accuracy on paperwork—far above the worth of any savings realized should the paperwork have contained an error.

Marks and Spencer evaluated their campaign not so much in terms of the payroll-reduction dollars, but, more importantly, in qualitative gains: attention to value and morale.

Caution: Such results don't last forever, as Tom Peters verifies in *A Passion for Excellence*. When Marcus Sieff began his job as managing director of Marks and Spencer, he spent the first year, again, getting rid of paperwork. He eliminated 80 percent, or about 27 million pages, a year.

A second example: How did IBM Brazil achieve success against the paperwork epidemic?

In March 1982 IBM Brazil, under project leader Fabio Steinberg, launched a campaign against paperwork. *International Management* (November 1984) reports that IBM Brazil eliminated 2.5 million documents a year, including 450 forms. They also threw away 50 unnecessary procedures. During the first phase of the program, they destroyed four tons of paper.

How did they spot the inefficiencies? Suggestions came from about one-fourth of the 4,000 employees in Brazil. But the cost of this massive reduction in paper was only a secondary matter. Management says the important result was the change in attitude among employees relieved of the excessive paperwork burden.

Then IBM CEO John Opel, at the parent company in New York, expressed equal commitment at IBM in the U.S. to get rid of red tape by writing an article published in the company's in-house magazine, which underscored top-management support.

To kick off the major campaign to cut paperwork, IBM Brazil hired a PR firm. They plastered the premises with attention-getting posters containing big red X's. They provided red X stickers for readers to slap on gobbledygook-filled documents that arrived on their desks. These documents were returned to the writer for clarification. The company coined slogans such as "Your word is worth a thousand memos" to imply trust and to eliminate the unnecessary written confirmations.

The degree to which employees participated in the paperwork reduction activities was considered when they received regular performance reviews.

As the IBM campaign exemplifies, the paperwork disease can be cured. But somebody with authority at the top has to approve the surgery. Any paper-reduction policy has to be initiated top-down and demonstrated by top management before others in the organization will cooperate on the cure. The lower-level and middle-level managers think that "somebody up there" requested the forms and reports they write. Therefore, senior executives have to be the ones to "unrequest" the paperwork.

So much for the paperwork-reduction and morale boost to the company as a whole. But what about you, the individual reader of this book? What do you have to gain by initiating or joining the effort to cut paperwork in your company?

First, you learn improved methods of management. For example, you learn how to keep communication flowing through the organization, how to maximize writing efforts, and how to get rid of morale problems caused by excessive administrative clerical tasks. Second, you are more visible to top management. Through less frequent, but more to-the-point, more useful communication with these top executives, you get your ideas heard and you get recognition for those ideas. Third, you lower your own operating and support-staff budget. Fourth, your people can become more productive, using their time where it counts—such as on improved customer service and creative product development. Fifth, you get action quicker. The more paperwork the longer the wait for action.

Can individual managers, then, motivated for personal as well as organizational reasons, really do much to cure their own departments of paper disease? Yes.

They specifically can best ask for their own departments, "Is this procedure really necessary? Can we combine it with another operation? Can we risk not doing it? Am I entrusting to the right people authority and responsibility for keeping the paperwork flowing on target? Do we solicit staff suggestions for changes in procedures, forms design, correspondence and report formats to eliminate the unnecessary, and rework the necessary, documents?"

Department managers, in effect, can begin to think like top management, seeing the "big picture" for their own departments.

Finally, let me assure you that I'm not saying you can or should eliminate all paperwork. However, for some departments that may be entirely possible and appropriate. On one occasion, while conducting a writing workshop for system engineers at IBM, I gave an overnight assignment for participants to revise a memo they'd previously written and to be prepared to distribute "before and after" copies the next day. One participant, in making his presentation the following day, confided that he didn't have the "before" half of the assignment; despite the fact that he'd been with the company six years, he'd never written a memo, letter, or report of any kind!

Rather than advocating the elimination of *all* paperwork, I'm suggesting that organizations eliminate the unnecessary:

- Customary cover letters that say only, "I'm sending you something; you have it in your hand now"
- Memos written as self-protection
- Forms that collect duplicate information

- Reams of computer printouts of information that has to be interpreted before it's usable
- Reports that are requested but never read
- Routine activity and trip reports
- Distribution lists that include everyone who's anybody with any possibility of the need-to-know by the year 2000
- Fifty-page documents sent to a manager who wants only a page of conclusions and recommendations
- Policy and procedure manuals that outline responses to every contingency possible
- Checks and balances that are meant to uncover errors that are far less expensive than the paperwork effort to correct them

Eliminate the unnecessary, cumbersome internal paperwork so that you can put your paperwork time where it counts—on documents your *customers* will see and use. Some organizations do just the opposite. Rather than focus their efforts on effective paperwork directed to the customer, they gag themselves on internal correspondence and then send "form" documents to their customers and clients!

So much for the costs, causes, and results of the paper disease; let's focus on the cure.

1

MANAGEMENT
STYLE
AND PAPER

RECOMMENDATION: REASSESS YOUR MANAGEMENT
STYLE TO SEE HOW MUCH UNNECESSARY PAPERWORK
YOU CREATE FOR YOUR STAFF AND YOURSELF. THEN
CHANGE THE PSYCHOLOGICAL FORCES AT WORK THAT
INFECT YOU WITH PAPER.

WHY STYLE HAS SUBSTANCE

Employees too often learn by examples of managers who play with paper to keep busy. Managers are supposed to think, make decisions, act. In the absence of these more taxing responsibilities, managers sometimes shuffle paper to delay the decision-making process and its resultant risks or to avoid making decisions altogether.

Business Week (January 24, 1977) cites one ousted CEO who permitted paperwork to paralyze his company: Then-chairman Franklin M. Jarmin, of Genesco, Inc., made one of his primary goals to set up a system of financial controls over the $1 billion retailing business. These controls, which became a personal obsession according to his closest employees, were his downfall. He paralyzed the company with his demand for paperwork. He asked for more and more details for every project and then sat on his decisions for weeks and even months. When he went on vacation, his top executives, using their stacks of memoranda as evidence of his paralyzing management style, met with the board and were successful in getting him fired.

11

To cite one example: CEO Jarmin had demanded a 75-page report on a new store they were opening. The report contained such trivial details as where to put the water coolers and whether they should have only cold water or both hot and cold. In fact, the company slogan was similar to what we still hear today in numerous departments of U.S. organizations: "Better run it by Frank."

Psychological Forces at Work on Managers

So how do many managers handle their insecurities?

Some *document*. They do not want to be held accountable for anything. Therefore they establish elaborate controls and systems for everything done in their department. They document every phone conversation and have subordinates send them enormous volumes of paperwork to document everything they've said or done. All to prove that these managers aren't responsible if things go wrong.

Some managers *delay*. They record all their thoughts on paper and distribute paper upward and laterally to get help and possibly to get someone else to make the decision before they are forced to do so.

Some managers *delegate*. They send all their paperwork downward, asking subordinates to gather more and more information and send more and more reports to keep them busy analyzing the situation "until all the facts are in." The trouble is that all the facts rarely ever come in. But as long as everybody below is busy, thinking the reason for delay is his or her own long-awaited report, then no one has to risk taking action and making a mistake. The whole department feels safe.

Delegating managers also tend to be overly impressed with jargon-spouting "experts" on their staff. Much of what these experts say is unintelligible, but the managers ask no questions; they are so impressed with the knowledgeable-sounding report that it's passed up the ladder without question. Of course, if someone else up the line does question, then the manager is not responsible—he or she has the subordinate's "misleading" report and is holding that subordinate "completely responsible."

Those supervisors, however, may resent managers' attempts to get comprehensible paperwork. A Ph.D. data-processing analyst at a public utility company recently complained when he entered one of my writing workshops: "My boss took this course a few months ago. Things have been kind of tough on me since. Yeah, I used to give him all these technical explanations, and he'd just accept what I said and send the report on. Now that he knows that's not good writing, he makes me put it in English. And he argues with me now that he knows what I'm saying."

Some managers *do*. They act and then record on paper what they've done as an afterthought. They ignore most of the paperwork that comes to them, therefore making uninformed decisions on "gut" reactions. At least they can't be accused of not taking action—of not "managing." But their subordinates grow more and more frustrated by information requested of them but then ignored.

Self-confidence, accountability, and excellent managerial skills all aid in curtailing these forays into paperwork.

Psychological Forces at Work on Subordinates

New employees, especially, feel the need to prove themselves. Much like the new graduate student trying to impress a professor, new employees feel the need to prove that they can handle the job and take on the new assignments. How do these employees prove themselves? Thoroughness—all captured in lengthy, jargon-filled documents that explore every possible aspect of a situation to the nth degree.

I once dealt with a young engineer new to his company who kept arguing with my suggestion that he present his conclusions and recommendations up front in his reports. His repeated response was that because he was new he had to first convince the boss that he knew what he was talking about by laying the appropriate groundwork before getting to the real point of the communication.

I don't think I would have ever persuaded him to do otherwise except for the finale of the workshop. The president of the company and several regional directors flew in for a cocktail party at the close of the two-day training class. During that cocktail hour, while the young engineer and I were talking, his regional director joined us, draped his arm over the engineer's shoulder, and turned to me: "Well, did you teach him to cut all the crap and get to the point, to just tell me what he wants me to do right up front?"

In addition to the need for new employees to prove themselves by presenting voluminous detail, some subordinates send their bosses lots of paper as self-protection. That is, they have the old gut reaction learned in sibling survival: Whenever father asks in a loud voice, "Who's been playing with my golf clubs?" the resounding chorus from the kids is "not me." In the business world most employees write their "not me" memos in advance of the accusations—just in case.

Another reason subordinates write long reports and send lots of printouts is that they are unsure of their own conclusions and recommendations. Thus, they force the boss to read through all the data as a doublecheck. Then, if somewhere down the line the conclusions turn out to be invalid, the subordinate has the boss, who read the report without questioning, out on a limb with him.

Still a fourth reason employees send their managers paper is simply to ask for reassurance: "Am I on the right track?" or "Am I doing a good job?" or "Can you give me some attention?"

HOW TO ALTER YOUR MANAGEMENT STYLE TO CURE THE DISEASE

How do you begin to cure the paper disease that infects your department's employees and creates misery and time-management problems for you?

Give Your People a Challenge

When people have too little to do, they think of ways to look busy, too often by pushing paper from their desk to yours or from their desk to their peers' desks.

They write memos to the file on every phone conversation. They decide to rewrite the policy manuals for their areas of responsibility. They establish tighter controls and more forms. They write detailed activity reports—everything you never wanted to know about the routine duties they perform each month. They design new forms to take the place of old forms, simply because they're old forms. They think of new ways to take data from computer printouts and turn it into new reports.

Instead of this substitute for meaningful work, give your employees projects they can bite into without having to play busy.

And if you're overstaffed, say so.

Create a Climate of Trust

When things go wrong, the first question should be, "What (not who) is the cause?" and the answer to that question will lead you to answer the next, "How should we fix it?" Answer the first question only as a springboard; focus on the second question. Verify assumptions, and be sure you have adequately defined the problem before generating paperwork as a solution.

In interview after interview when I asked professionals what kind of writing they think is unnecessary and should be eliminated within their organizations, they cited memos and reports to "cover" themselves.

The president of a subsidiary of Kaiser Aluminum explained to several of his top-level people the climate he wanted to produce throughout the company: "We trust you; if we didn't trust you, we wouldn't have hired you." Although he had made the comment to impress upon them the importance of concise writing, his comment should also have eased the minds of those writing self-protective memos for the files and to their bosses.

As long as a manager's first reaction is to point a finger, his or her employees will put far too many things in writing for self-protection.

Some managers create so many check-backs that they defeat even noble efforts at cost-cutting, all because they don't trust employees to help them cut costs without looking over their shoulder. To cite one example: When a company delivery vehicle was involved in a traffic accident, the safety officer had to go to the police station to get a copy of the accident report. The police charged $2 for the copy of the report, which the safety officer paid for personally. In the past, when such was the case, the safety officer had reported his out-of-pocket expense to the delivery supervisor on duty, who in turn reimbursed the safety officer and charged the amount on his daily expense report.

But because of new "cost-cutting" measures, the safety officer had to have special approval for all expenditures from his boss. Thus, he filled out a form to get his boss's approval on the $2 he'd already spent. Then the procedure called for the boss to send the form to the second-level manager in a city 30 miles away for a second approval signature. When that second-level manager approved the expenditure, he returned the form to the original office. With that proper approval, then the first manager filled out another form to refund the safety officer's $2. To make sure the $2 was a necessary expense, the company spent approximately $40 of employees' time for checks and balances.

And "cost-cutting" steps such as those just described do not even begin to assess the cost of employee morale. As the safety officer related the story, he added, "Usually, I just pay for things like that myself—like a 40-cent part I have to stop for at the auto-parts store." A bystander listening to the retelling of the incident added, "I guess that's how the company is saving so much money with this program. They get the employees to pay for enough things out of their own pockets rather than to go through the time and hassle of filling out the forms."

You don't have to observe a company long to feel the heavy blanket of distrust. Disgruntled employees talk. On a recent 15-hour visit to a large international oil company, I overheard the following remarks, all from different employees in different departments:

- "Better watch that Coke. You spill some on the carpet and you're in trouble. They'll cut the circle out and make you replace it out of your next paycheck. Or send you up to the 16th floor and have you stand with your nose in a circle on the wall. They have portable circles, too."
- "Here [taking document from me], I'll have to make the copies for you. We'll have to go up to the next floor and get the counter. They count everything around here. You fill out a form for *eve-ry-thing*. We count *eve-ry-thing*."
- "It really doesn't do too much good to get to the point around here. I work for a boss who'll rewrite it and fill it with so much BS before he passes it up that you won't believe it when you read it."
- "You don't do anything around here without writing a memo for approval. I just told my boss all this in a meeting [holding a memo toward me], and then he says 'write it.'"

The lack of trust (or the perception thereof) works against the organization in a thousand other ways. The CEO of a large banking corporation reiterated to me, just before a training session, his frustration in continuing to get 70-page loan analyses when all he wanted was a one-page analysis and recommendation. Later, when I posed the question, "Why do you write 70 pages instead of a short 'yes' or 'no'?" to a group of vice presidents, senior vice presidents, and executive vice presidents, I got a quick answer: "Fear."

Consider the high cost of low morale. As the best seller *In Search of Excellence* was about staying close to the customer, *A Passion for Excellence* was about trusting your employees. Train them; then trust them.

Get Out of Your Office and See What's Going On

Practice the MBWA (management by wandering around) philosophy described in *In Search of Excellence* and in its sequel, *A Passion for Excellence*. If you're out there with your staff, you won't need so many memos and reports to let you know what's going on. You won't have to wade through reams of computer printouts distributed en masse. You won't have to sit in meeting rooms where subordinates turn their paperwork into overhead transparencies and slides to tell you what's happening. Additionally, your perception of the whole will become more realistic. Paperwork can hide a lot of problems, or at least downplay them so that you literally have to read between the lines to know what's really going on with a particular customer or with a departmental project.

Now, the above point may seem obvious, but let me mention one example offered by an internal management consultant. Top executives of a Houston oil company called on their training department to help them with a morale problem. Although the company's operating capital had been riddled by legal battles, these top executives sensed something else sapping the energy and enthusiasm of their employees. The internal communication consultant spent several hours with these executives in one-on-one discussions suggesting they get up and walk around the halls and talk to people.

The response from these executives: "We have an open-door policy; people know they can come by to talk." Can you believe that? Either these top executives were fooling themselves, or they'd had their heads buried in their paperwork for the last 20 years.

Let Employees Think for Themselves

How often do you really need to be updated on the projects for which you demand weekly or biweekly reports? Do you read them immediately, or do they sometimes lie on your desk until the next report arrives? A marketing analyst estimates that she spends about six hours a week preparing a weekly report to management containing information that she says is already available in other formats. In fact, she uses these other reports to assemble her information. Those six hours, she insists, could be spent much more profitably out selling. Forty-three percent of those responding "yes" to my survey question about "unnecessary" reports say these reports are duplicates of information already available elsewhere.

Instead of burdening your employees with so many check-backs, consider having them do only "exception" reporting. That is, when what they have done, or are investigating, is routine, why have them write to you? Instead, encourage them to bring to your attention those things that they need further direction on or those things that you may want to be alerted to for other reasons.

And when they do report results to you, don't be hesitant to force them to interpret what they've said. Don't be impressed with gobbledygook or jargon, which is most often a hedge for an absence of real thinking and interpretation. Rather than picking up the pieces of their technical work for them and then rewriting the report so that it's useful to the next manager up the line, lead your subordinates to think through their information themselves.

You'd be surprised—or maybe you wouldn't—how many writers of long reports, and short memos as well, simply can't answer the question I often pose to them in private consultations on their writing: "Just what exactly is it that you want to say here?" They often can't tell me!

As a manager, don't settle for such sloppy work. Don't do subordinates' thinking. Guide, yes. Rewrite, no.

Give Recognition to Achievements Not Recorded on Paper

Some managers give the impression that they judge activity by the mounds of paper subordinates send to their desk. In casual conversations, in performance appraisals and in staff meetings, make sure that you recognize all work being done—whether or not you have paper in hand. When is the last time you complimented someone for handling an angry customer on the phone? When was the last time you complimented a salesperson on taking an extra 30 minutes to build goodwill with a customer—goodwill that didn't show up on the current period's sales record? When was the last time you commented on the extra effort a lower-level manager spent in grooming a subordinate for promotion? When was the last time you paid a bonus to someone for a new product or service idea not submitted to you in writing?

Reward Good Writing

Don't be satisfied just to have "something" on paper. Make sure that that "something" is presented to you in readable, usable form. Compliment subordinates not only on *what* they say, but also on *how* they say it.

A manager at a public-utility company had been trying for several months to get something done about an engineering problem, but the documents evidently were so poorly written that they got no action. After participating in a writing workshop and revamping the whole document, the engineer-manager sent it back to the vice president. Several days later the vice president caught him on the elevator and commented, "That's one of the best proposals that's crossed my desk in a long time." The writer immediately phoned the training director to pass along the compliment.

Do you think that employee will send junk to the VP again?

Some employees have the idea that nothing matters as long as the facts are given "somewhere in there." In fact, you can trace that misconception to the schoolroom question often asked of the teacher: "Are you grading on mechanics or just on content?"

In addition to rewarding employees by daily or weekly comments, reward them in annual performance appraisals by citing examples of excellent writing. Likewise, performance-appraisal comments on improvements needed in writing skills can also motivate an employee to seek help on his or her own time.

Finally, when you can, reward with bonuses. Sales managers give bonuses for sales in excess of quotas and frequently for referrals. If someone on your staff consistently produces good, concise, *necessary*, effective proposals to customers, consider a bonus.

Take Talk Seriously

Do your employees have to beat you over the head with paper before you give their concerns full consideration? A marketing representative had tried to get his manager's attention about a lack of proper inventory controls and constant delays in processing orders on the correct ship dates. He had discussed the problem with the boss on the phone, had put a message to him on his electronic message system, and had also mentioned the problem in a staff meeting. But the boss had given him no response whatsoever.

After expressing his frustration to me, the sales representative finally sighed, "I guess what I'm going to have to do is put it in a formal letter to him. That's the only way anybody ever gets his attention."

Why create extra reading for yourself by ignoring talk?

Reward Ideas to Cut Paper

According to researcher Dr. Martha Rader, the city of Phoenix gave an employee a $1,000 bonus for his idea to cut a routine periodic report from 35 pages to one. The suggestion saved the city $29,000 the first year alone.

When subordinates ask "why," listen. And if you can't come up with a good reason for compiling a report, sending out a course announcement, or supplying printouts, then reevaluate.

Awareness goes a long way in cutting paper, so:

- When you yourself start to write, ask why you're writing. If you don't like what your answers say about you, don't write.
- When your subordinates send you something you don't understand the value of, ask your subordinates why they wrote. Make them think twice before sending you more meaningless paper.
- Ask your boss "why?" when he or she asks you for a report. If the report is really necessary, the boss's answer will help you to make the report useful. If the boss can't tell you why, you probably don't need to write.

Don't Behead the Bearer of Bad Tidings

Some managers get good news in person and on paper, but they get bad news *only* on paper. Their employees have learned, like messengers to the proverbial king, that the wrath of the manager may be directed at the messenger rather than at a more appropriate target. If things are going badly in your company and in your division, that may be the reason for the pile of paperwork on your desk; those printouts or documents may be written so that you are forced to interpret the bad news for yourself.

Be careful that your body language, even in the absence of words, doesn't discourage the employee who reports bad news in person rather than on paper. Bad news is bad news however you learn it.

Don't Hide Bad News from Your Own Superiors

Likewise, have the courage to send up bad news yourself when it's called for, even though there are writing consultants who suggest that with sensitive information, perhaps writers should hold back the bottom-line message in reports they send up and instead break the news gradually.

Managers who insist that their subordinates use certain words that *sound good* (whether or not they are accurate) convey to their employees the idea that it doesn't make any difference if their writing doesn't say anything. They write "temporary solutions" instead of "bad past decisions"; "less significant advances" instead of "losses"; "systems failure" instead of "fraud"; "not totally unexpected sales trends" instead of "inaccurate forecasts." Because of this verbal sleight-of-hand, important decisions are sometimes based on informationless, inaccurate documents.

Again, we're discussing the matter of self-confidence, security, and a climate of trust. When subordinates see their managers pale and try to bury the facts when having to send up bad news, they'll do likewise in their communication to you, the manager.

Take Risks; Think Positively

True, no one can say what paperwork will be needed five years in the future. But you can't operate for long on the premise "We might as well keep a copy" before you create the kinds of records-retention costs mentioned in the Introduction. Remember those four file drawers of storage per employee at an annual maintenance cost of $2,160 each.

In addition to taking risks about what to save, take risks about what to verify. Productivity experts cite numerous studies showing that many people spend hours verifying and confirming data when the effort is far more costly than any mistake they may uncover.

Be aware of the cost of double-checking. Forget perfection on paper. Aim to get it right the first time and then think positively.

"Uh, this is not exactly the approach I had in mind."

2
THE WRITE/
EDIT/
REWRITE SYNDROME

RECOMMENDATION: AVOID THE WRITE/EDIT/REWRITE,
WRITE/EDIT/REWRITE SYNDROME FROM LAYER TO
LAYER, DEPARTMENT TO DEPARTMENT THROUGHOUT
THE ORGANIZATION.

A secretary from one of the nation's largest oil companies shook her head as she confessed to having typed the tenth draft of a 30-page memo on a new company policy. Her boss gave her a rough draft, which she typed and he edited. She retyped the edited version and then sent it to three other members of the policy committee, who each made comments for changes. She retyped the report. Then they as a team sent their draft to the manager, who made extensive changes before the secretary was asked to retype it. When that manager was satisfied, he passed it up to his boss, who also asked for changes before sending it out to other divisions for their comments. And so on. Ten drafts.

Can you imagine how much this cost the company? And I'm not talking about only clerical time for typing. I'm also talking about all the reading, re-reading, and revising time each employee spent on the document.

And this write/edit/rewrite activity is a common symptom of paper disease. In my survey of companies, these employees estimate that routine documents are "handled," on the average, 4.2 times within the organization before they reach the intended audience.

My survey respondents estimate that they spend 54 minutes preparing (planning, composing, and editing) the average memo or letter and three and three-quarter hours preparing the average report of two and a quarter pages. (The Dartnell Corporation's annually published figure of the average letter dictating time is seven minutes. This figure assumes, of course, that dictators get it right the first time and do no rewrites.)

Let's say Joe Jabberwrite earns $35,000 a year, or $17.50 per hour:

Joe's writing the average report of 2 1/4 pages   = $ 65.62
Joe's report-writing task annually (50 weekly reports)   = $ 3,281.00
Joe's writing the average letter or memo (54 minutes)   = $ 15.75
Joe's letter/memo writing cost annually (1 per week)   = $ 787.50
Organization's annual writing cost for 1,000 employees
($17.50/hour) who write at least one 2 1/4 page report
and one short memo or letter per week   = $4,068,500.00

*Above calculations do not even consider clerical support time in typing, duplicating, or distributing—or reading time for those on the distribution list.

And this kind of write/edit/rewrite waste is going on at every level of most organizations.

Why?

MISAPPLICATION OF THE "COMPLETED STAFF WORK" IDEA

Completed staff work, in essence, means that when a subordinate is given an assignment he or she should not bother the boss with questions until the project is completed.

Where writing is concerned, that means something close to the following: An employee begins with the problem, investigates the options for solutions, decides on the best course of action, prepares all necessary documents required to initiate that action, and then submits his or her work to the supervisor so that all that remains to be done (if the supervisor agrees with the proposed solution) is for the supervisor to sign the necessary documents to put the solution into force.

Completed staff work, of course, does have advantages: The boss has to deal with the problem only twice—when assigning the project and when approving its completion. The boss doesn't get bogged down in detail but instead is free to manage the overall picture. The subordinate learns to think through problems thoroughly and to develop personal time-management and decision-making skills. The subordinate takes responsibility for his or her own work.

Although it sounds good and works well in the decision-making, problem-solving part of the project, completed staff work wastes considerable time, of both supervisor and subordinate, when it comes to the writing or documentation of projects. Why should an employee spend 40 hours putting a proposal or report together, only to hand it to the supervisor and have him or her say, "That's not what I had in mind"? Then both supervisor and writer must spend additional time discussing the answers to questions that they both should have determined long before the employee got to the writing stage.

Yes, employees should "think through" the problem and proposed solutions. They should make sure they know the *why* of the project, define the problem correctly, recheck all facts, eliminate unsupported generalizations, investigate all options, and explore the effects of the suggested solutions.

But the completed staff work idea should stop at the point of putting all this work on paper. At that point, the employee will do well to sketch out a "skeleton" outline and give the boss (or others on the project who have input and veto power) opportunity for feedback on the approach *before* the writer commits ideas to paper in final form. Why?

When I ask writers why they think their boss makes changes in their writing, most say the changes are a result of the boss adding, deleting, or clarifying information. In other words, these changes would be unnecessary if the boss had given adequate background and preview of the project assigned to the subordinate.

Professional writers and their publishers know better than to try to operate along the lines of completed staff work as defined earlier. Instead, authors outline their novel, nonfiction book, or magazine article and have the editor accept it or make changes at the outline stage before investing time in a complete manuscript. The time of the subordinates and the manager/editor is no less valuable.

Reviewing an *outline* to determine required changes and additional ideas to be incorporated is much quicker than reading a complete draft, then asking for changes, and then rereading the revised document. Before having subordinates give you a final draft of a complex report or proposal going outside the company or up the organization, do an outline review and give feedback before you both have to do your work twice.

GIVE ADEQUATE BACKGROUND INFORMATION

Mass mailers don't send their advertisements to everyone. More sophisticated marketing techniques and research enable them to target special audiences; with this background, advertisers tailor their messages to specific groups. Yet managers often fail to provide available, essential background to their subordinates, thus virtually guaranteeing an unfocused document.

According to a survey conducted by Louis Harris & Associates, Inc. for Steelcase, Inc. (reported by Debra Haskell in *Modern Office Procedures,* September 1979) 74 percent of all white-collar workers say they could do more in a day than they usually accomplish. One of the primary reasons cited for low productivity is inadequate instruction by their bosses.

In explaining why apology letters often are edited six or eight times before they go out to the patients or relatives of patients at a Houston hospital, a staff person responsible for answering complaints says:

> "The problem with writing here at the hospital is that the complaint usually goes down to the person with the lowest level of knowledge about the whole thing. But instead of each person's passing background information down to me to use in my response, they only pass down the complaint. Then when I write the letter and send it back up the chain, all these people edit and add comments, attaching this or that piece of information that sheds new light on the situation. What I can't figure out is why they don't tell me all I need to know before I write the letter the first time?"

They should.

A manager who asks someone to prepare a document to send up the chain or out of the organization should always give the writer the following information:

- *Audience*—Who will read the document and for what purpose?
- *Special Problems Involved*—Will there be skepticism about the information? Will there be political problems that mandate tactful wording? Will there be situational problems that require special deadlines, special distribution, special processing of the information?
- *Background Issues*—What past decisions or related information may have a bearing on how the situation is handled?

- *Time Frame*—How long will the writer have to pull together the information? A week? Eight hours? Or do you want the information yesterday? Don't force your subordinate to meet unrealistic deadlines. He or she may do significant research to compose a meaningful document and then tarnish the entire effort by having to put together the report under impossible deadlines. Not only are you sabotaging the project, you're creating severe frustration for the subordinate. He knocks a homerun ball out of the park and you call time out before he can run the bases! If there's a tight deadline, at least say so at the beginning.
- *Resources*—What prerogatives does the writer have about final decisions? What resources are at his or her disposal? Will you pull rank for the necessary staff and monetary support?
- *Reviews*—Tell the writer what you want in the way of checkbacks. When should he or she come to you with questions about proposed solutions and costly investigations?

Finally, don't negate all these good instructions by giving them in such haste that the writer can't comprehend. In other words, you can't delegate a major writing task as you walk out the door at 4:30 on Friday afternoon while jangling your car keys. If the document is important enough to be written, it's important enough to set a specific time to discuss all the necessary information.

When you're the writer preparing a document for someone who doesn't provide the above information, learn to be an interrogator. Don't start to write until you know the answers to these questions, or you might as well whip out your calendar and immediately schedule rewrite time.

STIFLE THE URGE TO EDIT FOR EDITING'S SAKE

You'd be surprised how many managers think they haven't done their job if they haven't made a few changes in the letters, memos, or reports prepared by subordinates before these managers forward them up the ladder or out of the organization. In fact, their compulsion to edit is so strong that subordinates tell me they often leave red herrings in their work so that managers will have something to edit out and can leave the "good stuff" alone.

In fact, someone has said: "The greatest passion in the world is not love or hate, but the compulsion to change another man's copy." Edit a subordinate's writing only for good (and explicable) reasons.

If you're asked to edit a peer's writing project, make sure you know what you're supposed to be reviewing. Are you supposed to be looking for missing details? Feasibility of ideas? Or simply grammatical errors? If you don't know your purpose for the review, find out before you edit.

DETERMINE A HIERARCHY OF VALUES FOR EDITING

All the above is not to say that managers never need to edit or that peers never need to make changes in writing submitted by one of their group. Instead, it is to say that managers should edit only to the extent that they can justify the changes for the intended purpose and importance of the document.

Learn the differences between writing, editing, and rewriting: *Writing* involves the thinking process behind a document as well as composition of the document. *Editing* involves marking unclear or grammatically incorrect phraseology and raising questions about vague or missing ideas, gaps in logic, or inaccuracies. The document is returned to the writer for another look and possible rewrite. Finally, *rewriting* is a complete overhaul; the editor/manager uses the original writer's ideas perhaps but makes all the changes himself or herself. You can easily understand the irritation managers create for themselves when they think it's their duty to rewrite their subordinates' documents.

Another danger—a side effect you might say—of this edit/rewrite, edit/rewrite syndrome is that people who rewrite often unintentionally change the meaning of a sentence when they intend only to correct a stylistic or grammatical error. In addition to the manager's time involved in editing and the danger of changed meanings, the writer, too, feels more and more frustrated about his work. As a result, the manager continues to get worse and worse copy to edit. I've run across many employees who confess, "Oh, I just send up the first draft—just anything; he (or she) is going to rewrite it anyway."

And more than a few writers never learn what it is that the manager finds wrong with their writing. In fact, when subordinates were asked why their bosses make editorial changes, 40 percent of my survey respondents gave comments such as "no reasons," "personal preference," "ego," "not invented here," or "don't know." Managers themselves cited their reasons for changes as "clarity," "organization," "lack of focus," "grammar," or "addition of more information."

Clearly, managers and subordinates are not communicating—with each other, never mind the intended reader at the other end.

So think before you yield to the temptation to edit. Managers' editorial changes usually fall into one of the following categories: content, organization, clarity, grammar, conciseness, style.

In my hierarchy of values, the first three and a half are "must" changes; the last two and a half are the finer points to be addressed after the writer has mastered the others.

To explain:

Content

Certainly, manager-editors need to raise questions about missing or incorrect details and facts. They may need to suggest a graph rather than a column of figures for better illustration of production trends. They may question the necessity of including four paragraphs about rust corrosion when that problem is rare on the proposed model. Finally, the facts have to be accurately presented.

Organization

The organization of the content is important for the clarity and usefulness of the document to the intended audience. In fact, a disorganized presentation of facts is probably the greatest hindrance to clarity.

Note what I mean with the following two memos:

Version 1

Gerri,

Revenue brought this to me. Apparently, Blendwold billed us for $154.05 for a joint-venture payout correction on Baytree #1. I had Sandra check on this, and she couldn't find this billing in October or November 198-. Accordingly, Blendwold did not get paid, so they subtracted this amount from the revenue. It took them two checks to do that (see August & September 198- billings).

Revenue wants us to make an entry to get it off their books. Can you see if this was ever paid? If not, can you have it approved and sent back to me so that I can make an entry? If you have any questions, please call.

Version 2

Gerri,

Blendwold Company did not get paid for a joint-venture payout correction billing (Baytree #1) dated December 198- for $154.05, so the company deducted this bill from our revenue checks. Revenue wants us to make an entry to correct our books.

> Would you please check to see if this bill was ever paid? If this bill has not been paid, please have it approved and sent back so that I can make an entry to clear Revenue's books.
>
> I had Sandra check on this, and she could not find where the invoice has been paid in either October or November 198-. Because this bill was a correction, it could have been sent further into 198-. I have enclosed copies of the bill and copies of documents showing the expenses subtracted from revenue. It took Blendwold two checks to make the correction: August 198- and September 198-.

In the first memo, the real point is buried at the end of the document and most readers won't know how to "process" the details until they get to the last paragraph. Therefore, such clumsy organization causes readers to have to review the document twice; when they finally get to the ah-ha sentence, they go back and reread the details and reprocess them in light of the real message. (For more on proper organization, see Chapter 7.)

Therefore, editing for organizational changes or missing or incorrect detail is appropriate.

Clarity

Additionally, managers should edit for clarity. When you read a sentence such as:

> "Procedures should be established by October 1."

the manager/editor should rightly ask, "By whom?" This passive-voice sentence leaves out the doer—who should establish the procedures? This information is probably obvious in the mind of the writer, who is familiar with the situation, but unclear to the reader.

Grammar

Managers should edit for any grammatical errors that reflect badly on the image of the company or the writer, as well as for grammatical errors that lead to clarity problems. (Most grammatical errors *do* cause misreading.) You'll notice earlier that in my hierarchy of values for editing I referred to this category of grammar by halves.

Gross grammatical errors call for correction; minor ones may not be worth the cost involved in the rewrite. That's not to say that I'm not a very conservative grammarian and that grammar is unimportant; it is to say that what some people think are grammar rules are really style matters.

Let me illustrate: I've seen many complete documents returned to the writer for a rewrite because of a sentence such as this:

These statistics should be sent to all division directors, managers, and other department heads.

Evidently, some writers were taught to put a comma before the *and* in a series like the one above; others were taught always to omit the comma.

The point is that the comma in such a series is truly optional. And although some sentences can be misread without the comma (the last two ideas may be taken as a unit—particularly in a technical subject), the sentence above cannot be misread, with or without the last comma in the series.

Do managers really edit for such minor points as this? You bet. In one incident, the president of a company sent out a memo to all employees instructing them that they should not use a comma before the coordinate conjunction when both clauses are short. Example: "He left at noon and he returned at 2:30." Should you send out a memo or ask a writer to revise a letter for this? No!

To sum up about editing for grammar: Mark grammatical errors that reflect poorly on the company or that create clarity problems, but don't expect complete rewrites for such mistakes unless the document is indeed important—perhaps a proposal for a $1 billion contract.

Now to the matter of conciseness. For complete details, see Chapter 7. For our purpose here, let me assure you that conciseness is a matter of great concern for readers throughout the organization. When someone writes a two-page memo, going to a distribution list of 40 people, instead of a single-page memo, she probably has wasted about two hours' worth of company time and payroll.

Conciseness also ensures clarity. When writers give too much detail on a point, they blow a minor idea out of proportion to its importance in the big scheme of things. Careful organization, however, will prevent the problem.

But there are lapses in conciseness that managers must learn to overlook in the interest of time, money, and frustration. For example:

In order to lower our cost in operating these copiers, I am asking that you refrain from making copies for personal use.

Granted, "In order to lower" could be condensed to "To lower…" and "refrain from making copies for personal use" could be written "do not make personal copies." But are those changes worth the time and frustration of rewrite? I think not.

Style

Now to the last reason for editing—style. Think of style as your personal logo or your company logo. Style is the individual mark on your writing. Style involves choices such as:

Enclosed please find	vs.	Enclosed are...
Your business will be		
appreciated	vs.	We appreciate your business.
Pursuant to your request...	vs.	After your request...

Granted, the phrases on the right are more conversational and certainly convey a personal touch, which is the trend in business writing today. Those in the left column seem overly formal, stilted, and old-fashioned. But when editing, remember that your subordinate can master only one, or at most, a few things at a time. These kinds of changes should come further down on the hierarchy of values for editing.

Some style points, however, are strictly a matter of personal preference and should be left to the individual writer's discretion.

A lawyer writing a thank-you letter to another law firm outside his organization had used this sentence: "We are glad to have had the opportunity to work with you on this case." His manager had edited "glad" to "happy," and they had argued 45 minutes on the change. You can be sure they were really arguing over a symptom of a much larger problem—the frustration of continual editing and its effect on the writer.

Nevertheless, managers should learn the difference between editing for a reason and editing strictly because the document is not written the way they themselves would say things.

Yes, all the above considerations—content, organization, clarity, grammar, conciseness, and style are important. But managers need to develop their own hierarchy for editing so as to take care of first things first and to minimize frustration and the cost of excessive paperwork on the part of both manager and writer.

A few further guidelines on the mechanics of editing:

- Read the entire document before you start making comments about organization. Look at the overall layout to see that it is appropriate and the most advantageous for the purpose. Use checklists to help you remember and communicate to the writer what the weaknesses are.

- Don't employ sarcasm in your editing. You convey sarcasm by trying to obliterate with dark red pen the offensive words or paragraphs; a light pencil (not red) will do nicely. Avoid comments in the margin such as: "What the hell is this?" and "Haven't the foggiest notion what this means." Make suggestions for improvements, not just vague comments such as "fix it" (the total comment from one editor on one of my colleagues' first manuscripts). Allow your subordinate to ask questions about editorial comments you've made. How can you possibly expect him or her to repair something if the error or weakness is not clear? To drastically understate my point, sarcasm does not motivate an employee to write better.
- Don't hesitate to let subordinates know that you yourself revise things you write. So do professional writers. Judging from the habits of my author friends, I'd say most book manuscripts are the result of three or four drafts. To the more fastidious writers like Hemingway, who, according to tradition, revised *A Farewell to Arms* 17 times, perfection may never come. Nor is revising to that extent time-efficient. But do encourage writers to compare drafts and improvements.
- Let writers reap the benefits of their efforts in revision. Pass on good comments you hear from your subordinates, peers, or bosses.
- Lead a subordinate to question, evaluate, and edit his writing himself. Simply schedule a discussion to raise questions and permit the writer to tell you how satisfied he is about the writing.

Finally, remember that "enough is enough" on any editing. A staff consultant at a high-tech company directs the writing of internal documents that confirm agreements between two internal departments. He claims that often the two sides keep editing documents back and forth, watching and changing clauses that either increase or decrease their authority or responsibility until the document is no longer relevant and the total project to which the document referred has been completed. That's taking the write/edit/rewrite process to the point of ridiculousness.

A personnel director at a $3.5 billion energy company, concerned about excessive paperwork and the editing process, says he and his assistant traced a four-paragraph letter through the organization for 17 rewrites before it went to the intended audience.

Another employee tells of a project on which he and his group could not get the manager to sign off on their report without making changes. On the fourth try, just for a lark they decided to send the original draft.

The manager signed it without question.

Develop a hierarchy of values. You can't change everything every time.

ADOPT OR CREATE A COMPANY STYLE GUIDE

Retired Colonel Leonard S. Lee, internationally recognized expert on records management and systems analysis, estimates that national turnover in administrative positions is close to 30 percent annually (*Records Management Quarterly*, April 1982). Of course, this varies by industry from about 17 percent to about 44 percent, but whatever your company's attrition rate, how can you expect any new employee coming into the company to know what a particular manager or company prefers in writing styles or terms? Furthermore, in one study Lee cites, of a group of 1,000 people over a year's time, 565 employees transferred to different jobs *within* the company. In some companies, such a turnover, even within the same organization, means constant relearning of a manager's or department's writing peculiarities and preferences.

An ideal way to prevent some of the edit/rewrite, edit/rewrite frustrations and loss of time is to have all employees use the same style guide. In other words, somebody decides once and for all that you either capitalize the names of departments or that you don't. And that's that.

Many organizations that do have style guides haven't bothered to communicate that fact to all their employees who write. In fact, the style book is such a secret in some companies that only the "professional writers"—those in PR or in editorial departments—know that one exists. If the "average" employee who writes knew such style guides were available to answer questions about appropriate usage, some large organizations could eliminate several positions for people who do nothing but edit outgoing documents to make sure everything conforms to that guide—matters of comma usage, abbreviations, capitalization, etc.

If your organization does not have a style guide and if you don't want to invest the time and money in developing one, there are plenty of good ones already on the market.

Adopt one, ask a knowledgeable employee to add a small supplement for matters specific to your company, and then let people know what the adopted style book is. When there's a question, reference to such a guide is a lot quicker than a complete rewrite after the manager edits the comma in and the next reader edits it out.

3
THE
APPROVAL
PROCESS

RECOMMENDATION: LET YOUR EMPLOYEES "OWN"
THEIR WORK. SIMPLY ADD YOUR APPROVAL WITH AN
"APPROVAL SIGNATURE" LINE.

Let me say at the outset I'm not advocating that all CEOs and senior executives do away with their staff writers and ghostwritten letters, memos, or speeches. Writers who prepare documents for a boss's signature or presentation in these cases are *supposed* to adopt the boss's style; they are writing their *boss's* correspondence or speeches, not their own.

What this chapter refers to, rather, is the practice of having employees write documents that should be their own but that somehow get signed by the boss before they go up the chain of command for review and/or approval.

Here's an example of the approval process used by most companies: An accountant finds that buyers in various divisions are dealing with vendors not on the company's approved vendor list. He calls this irregularity to the attention of his boss and suggests that all buyers be reminded of the corporate policy about ordering supplies only from those vendors on the list. The boss agrees and asks the subordinate to prepare a memo on the problem, usually for the boss's signature. The boss signs the original memo and sends it along to a second-level manager, perhaps the controller. Then the controller asks the first-level manager to write a memo for the controller's signature to all purchasing agents in the company telling them to deal only with vendors on the approved list.

How would this document look with an approval signature? The accountant simply writes the ultimate-message memo to the boss with appropriate approval line(s)

Approved by ——————— Date —————
Approved by ——————— Date —————

underneath his or her own signature line.

If the boss approves, he or she simply signs it and passes the information on to the intended audience or the next person who has approval or veto authority. Obviously, this cuts down on paperwork in that it reduces a two- to four-memo process to one document and speeds up any action involved.

But the approval-line process, rather than the ghostwriting habit that involves multiple rewrites, has several advantages other than speed.

THE EDIT COMPULSION

First, the "for your signature" writing process immediately triggers managers to edit—not only for necessary reasons such as content, organization, or clarity, but also for personal preference in style matters. When the manager's name appears at the bottom of the document as the writer rather than simply as the approver she wants things said her way.

The surbordinate may have written,

"This letter will confirm our agreement to...."

The manager changes it to,

"I want to confirm our agreement to...."

The subordinate may have written,

"This arrangement will not end when the consultant's contract is completed; it implies an ongoing process."

The manager changes it to,

"This process will not end when the consultant's contract is completed. The situation implies an ongoing arrangement."

Although managers theoretically understand that there's more than one way to say anything, if their signature identifies them as writer, rather than just approver, they feel compelled to say things "the best way"—their way.

An approval line, however, lessens this editing-for-personal-preference compulsion. The manager realizes that other readers will attribute weaknesses or awkwardness in the wording to the originator of the document, not to him or her as approver.

RELEARNING FOR TRANSFEREES

With the approval-signature process, employees do not have to relearn the boss's style each time they transfer from one department or division to another—nothing new to most employees.

Of course, all the movers and transferees will need to examine good models for documents unfamiliar to them in either content or layout. But with the approval line rather than the "for your signature" approach, they will not additionally have to worry about how the boss wants things said.

If there is a major difference of opinion about how a document should be arranged or about special phrasing peculiar to a certain new department, then the writer should learn these differences immediately, before writing anything in the new department. Special writing "musts" should be part of the orientation for a new department or job. New employees should discuss writing do's and don't's with the boss at the same time that the boss gives them information about audience, purpose, special problems, and background for tackling their communication task.

RECOGNITION AND ACCOUNTABILITY

So how does writing for someone else's signature destroy respect for the individual and personal initiative? When was the last time you fixed a leaky faucet in your motel room? If you don't own things, don't get recognition, and don't receive any particular benefit, why should you spend the extra energy and time putting things right?

Numerous employees who attend my workshops bitterly complain about the fact that they get little recognition for what they write. Here's a comment—and a common complaint—from a staff analyst:

"By the time my report gets edited by three or four people before it gets to the top, I don't even recognize the thing as mine. There's not a sentence in there that's me."

Accompanying such a comment is usually a look of resentment, defeat, and resignation, all of which eventually lead to settling for mediocrity rather than to spending more energy on creative efforts on the company's behalf.

On the other hand, when writers see their work get the recognition it deserves—recognition outside the immediate department—they begin to gain enthusiasm for the job well done. Often, comments for outstanding reports or proposals, even though passed down through the ranks and back to the originator, go to the person who *signed* the document as his or hers rather than to the real author. The author may have the satisfaction of knowing that his boss knows that the contribution and praise belong to him, but the originator also knows that no one else up the corporate ladder will be able to link his name to his "baby."

In entry-level jobs, this anonymity may be known as part of paying one's dues. But the process of writing for someone else's signature doesn't stop with entry-level positions. To the detriment of the development of lower-level managers, some are still forced to write for the signature of the next higher-up.

Of course, recognition and accountability benefit the organization as a whole, not only the employee-writer. Writers become accountable for their own mistakes—in content, in problem-solving and persuasion, in clarity, in everything. The writer cannot have the attitude that "if it's not right" the manager will catch it.

That careless attitude, in effect, is delegating writing tasks to the boss. And managers, amazingly enough, often accept that delegation and do rewrites for their subordinates rather than simply approve or return the document for a rewrite.

Recognition and accountability benefit both employee-writer and the organization.

EMPLOYEE MORALE

In industry, 20 percent of the office workforce disappears each year; in government, that figure approaches 30 percent. Some may consider it

a long leap of logic to say that "for your signature" documents contribute to employee dissatisfaction and eventual resignation. So might
I—if I hadn't heard the following stories and many more like them:

An accountant at one of my client firms approached me about a job to
conduct workshops.

> "I have the necessary educational background to teach, and I'm
> also a good writer. In fact, I do practically all the writing for
> everything that goes out of my department. Everybody has learned
> that I enjoy writing and that I know what I'm doing because the
> manager keeps telling them to come ask me their questions. What
> really hacks me is that I'm making $25,000 a year to make a
> $60,000 manager look literate. His name goes on everything I do. I
> wouldn't mind the work. As I said, I enjoy writing. It's just that I'd
> like to have recognition for what I do—recognition from someone
> besides my manager."

A similar story: A rising-star-engineer-turned-manager at one of the
largest oil and gas companies in the nation resigned his position recently to accept an entry-level position in a much smaller company. His
explanation:

> "Frankly, it wasn't more money. On the contrary. I just got tired of
> carrying my boss's lunch. I did all the work, wrote the documenta-
> tion for his signature, and nobody ever knew I breathed there. At
> my new company, I'm more visible to the top executives. When I
> prepare a report or a proposal, my name goes on the work."

BETTER WRITING THE FIRST TIME

In addition to minimizing the edit compulsion, eliminating the
reeducation of transferees, giving recognition, establishing
accountability, and increasing job satisfaction in general, signing one's
own name to a document ensures that the manager gets better copy the
first time around. Writers frequently comment, "I don't bother anymore
with trying to get it right. There is no 'right.' Whatever I send up, the
boss is going to change. I just send up a first draft."

If the writer, on the other hand, knows that his or her work will simply be returned with sparse comments from the boss about changes for
the rewrite, chances are greater that the document will get more attention the first time. To cite the earlier-mentioned engineer: With

approval lines rather than documents prepared for the boss's signature, the manager lets the subordinate know that he or she need no longer "carry the lunch."

FOCUS ON THOSE WHO NEED HELP AND THOSE WHO NEED PROMOTION

Finally, with every employee responsible for his or her own writing, the company finds out who can communicate well and who can't. Those with good communication skills can then be promoted to where their skills can best be used.

A case in point: Jerry Murray began as an editor and technical writer at Exxon. But as she continued to edit for engineers, her skills as a writer far surpassed the skills of those she edited. When her contribution was recognized within the company, she left her position to teach technical-writing professionals within Exxon how to prepare better technical reports. Eventually, she became so good at what she did that she began her own consulting business.

If organizations don't want to lose their best employees by recognizing their skills, companies can offer incentives and give assignments suitable to those outstanding skills. Additionally, organizations can quickly pinpoint writing deficiencies in those they intend to promote into management circles. Because managers have increased responsibilities to communicate, companies can teach them writing skills before the managers are forced to latch onto a subordinate who may or may not be willing "to carry the lunch."

Lest you think using approval lines rather than simply having subordinates prepare documents for their managers' signatures is new, think again. The idea has been working quite well in some industries and situations for years.

For example, many organizations and agencies dealing with volumes of forms use the approval-only process. Spaces for the approver's signature or initials are provided on the form. An approval signature does not mean that the form is necessarily neatly typed with phrasing just as the approver would have chosen but rather that the information is accurate.

Finally, remember that an approval line rather than an entire document written anonymously for the manager's signature does not mean, necessarily, that the manager will approve everything that comes to him or her regardless of the quality of the writing. What use of the approval line does mean, however, is that the manager will not feel the compulsion to edit simply because it's not the way he or she would have said it.

Further, the *unsigned* approval line ensures that the manager will not do the rewrite. Instead, the rewrite is the responsibility of the originator of the document. If that employee has writing deficiencies, it's his or her responsibility to improve those communication skills before promotion time.

We're talking about accountability, not imitation. About pride in work well done. About respect for the individual. About ownership. All of which leave the manager free to manage.

4
THE
UBIQUITOUS
TRANSMITTAL

RECOMMENDATION: ELIMINATE 70 PERCENT
OF ALL THE TRANSMITTAL
LETTERS OR MEMOS YOU WRITE.

Approximately one-fourth of all letters and memos written are transmittals for reports, proposals or routine information requested from the
sender. Another one-fourth of the transmittals accompany information
routinely sent weekly, monthly or quarterly.

According to the Dartnell Institute of Business Research, in 1985 the
"average" letter of about 185-190 words composed in seven minutes
cost $8.52 dictated face to face and $6.22 dictated to a machine.

From my experience, that cost is a minimum for most letter writers.
The "special" letters or memos (those that are not routine and tackle
more sensitive or complex subjects) cost much more than the seven
minutes to compose and revise—according to estimates on my surveys,
an average of 54 minutes. Additionally, the cost of those written in
longhand and then typed is higher still. Besides writing, handling, and
retention cost, there are other reasons for eliminating ubiquitous transmittal documents.

WHY ELIMINATE ROUTINE TRANSMITTALS?

They're Superfluous

Most transmittals simply say, "I'm sending you something." If that's the sole purpose for the cover document, you're insulting your reader's intelligence. He or she can see that the "something" has arrived. Consider these actual transmittals (names, dates and numbers changed) from my files:

> Dear Sir:
> As requested in your letter dated December 3, 198-, I'm enclosing the blue warranty copy for invoice no. 0090-399.
> Sincerely,

> To: Distribution
> From:
> Please find attached information related to the upcoming Vinar Users meeting. Please contact me if you or your staff are interested in attending.

> Gentlemen:
> Enclosed please find copies of the Balar Trustee and Paying Agent Agreements distributed by Batton & Batton Company dated June 16, August 1, and September 8. Please advise if further information is needed.

> To: Distribution
> From:
> Enclosed for your information is a copy of the revised Oil and Gas Production Costs Summary for the month of December198-.

Why write these kinds of transmittal? Can't the reader see what's attached or enclosed?

They're Ignored

You may insist, "But the transmittals I send don't take any time or create unnecessary paperwork; they're form documents that we use every month (or every quarter) with this report."

If that's the case, then there's an additional reason to eliminate them. If they are form documents for routine reports or information, then the recipients know what information you're sending when they see it and they know not to bother to read the transmittal since it says the same thing each time.

For example, take the typical transmittal document for an internal audit report:

> Subject: Review of the Financial Operations of the XYZ Division of Flackfelt Products Company as of June 30, 198-
>
> We have completed review of the financial operations of the XYZ Division as of June 30, 198-. The income statement and balance-sheet account balances were prepared in accordance with the policies and procedures of the XYZ Division, a division of Flackfelt Products Company.
> While most account balances were found to be accurately stated, instances were noted where adjustments should be made to more accurately reflect the XYZ Division's operations for the three months ended June 30, 198-. Also, while many accounting and operating controls were found to be adequate, instances were noted where improvements should be made to strengthen existing controls and procedures. The findings are listed in the body of the enclosed report along with the recommendations.
> The review was performed by Sue Smith, Henry Jones, and Fred Cross. We sincerely appreciate the courtesies and assistance received from all personnel who participated in the review.

Now, tell me, what is said in the above transmittal that the reader doesn't or wouldn't know from glancing at the executive overview on the first page of the report? That the audit was performed according to standard procedures? Aren't they all? That the report contains recommendations? Don't they all? That Sue Smith, Henry Jones and Fred Cross did the work? Who cares? Do you have internal auditors doing audits that you don't trust? Do you appreciate the courtesies and assistance of others? Of course.

The reason for a *necessary* cover letter on a report may be to preview a summary of the report's findings. But no such summary is included in "typical" transmittals. Very few of the transmittals I see contain an informative overview of the attachment or enclosure. The 70 percent that I recommended eliminating look like the ones included here.

If you do need an *internal* transmittal for a periodic report or memo because you have to add at least one new twist to the information or the response, then use a form checklist. Simply fill in the varying date or response or ask for the missing detail by checking the correct box. Such a slight variation is not worth an original transmittal to accompany the routine document.

They're Repetitious

When a transmittal does contain a basic summary or executive overview of the information attached, at least it has a purpose in providing a synopsis for the skimming reader. But often the transmittal memo or letter is detached from the rest of the document by the first reader. Therefore, for safety and thoroughness, a writer should always include an overview or executive summary up front in the report or proposal itself.

And that, of course, makes most transmittals, even those with good overviews, repetitious—and unread.

They Contradict and Confuse

One of the first things technical writers learn is that they should say the same things in the same ways—exactly. For example, in the text of a technical report, an engineer should not refer to a "head and lever" pulley construction, and later in a drawing refer to the same construction as a "pulley device making use of a head and lever." Changing the name for something or changing the phrasing even slightly can confuse the reader.

Likewise with a cover letter. A writer states in the transmittal that "the deficiencies in the irrigation system merit careful attention." Then later in the report itself, the writer says that "the deficiencies, although they merit attention, are not serious drawbacks on which to base a buying decision." Such variations confuse the reader. Which to believe: the summary in the transmittal letter or memo or the summary in the report itself?

They Prevent Further "Selling"

If you've written a good transmittal that really says something besides "I'm sending you something," you often tempt your boss or your customer or client to stop reading with that transmittal. Had you omitted the transmittal letter or memo and instead begun your proposal or report with title page and executive summary, you might have persuaded the reader to continue through the document for more information—persuasive arguments for your ideas, service, or product.

Chapter endings in books have the same effect as transmittals; they're always looked upon by the reader as a good place to *stop* reading. Novelists learn to end a chapter with a "cliff hanger" or preview of what's to come. A transmittal often tempts the executive reader to stop, thinking he or she has the whole picture, whereas if the summary and executive overview are included as the beginning of the report or proposal, your top executive or client reader may be tempted to continue reading your sales pitch.

They Delay Responses

Consider how many hours or days a document lies on your desk or on that of your secretary waiting for a transmittal memo or letter to be typed to accompany it. Two hours? A day? Even a week while a secretary is on vacation or out ill?

Chances are the same thing is true of information you've requested from others. It's spending a couple of extra days on someone's desk waiting for an accompanying transmittal.

SO HOW DO YOU KNOW WHEN YOUR TRANSMITTAL IS NECESSARY?

Write a transmittal letter as a sales tool. If you eliminate most of your internal transmittals, you can take the extra time to compose a letter to a client or customer that sells.

When the occasion is too formal for a "buck" slip, then how about simply returning the original (or a copy of the original) letter or memo of request with the information you're forwarding?

This method certainly works fine with invoices. The receiver merely returns a copy of the invoice (either supplied by the seller or copied by the buyer) with payment to ensure correct crediting of his or her account.

The same principle is at work with the transmittal. Simply clip the memo, letter, or phone message note to the requested information and send it along. If there's any doubt that the requester won't know or remember what he or she has asked for, the attached original request will serve the purpose nicely.

For the more formal occasions when a buck slip or copy of the requester's document will not do, evaluate the need for a formal transmittal by asking the following questions:

1. Do you need a record of submission? That is, do you need a file record of the submission date and the name of the recipient of the information? Are you sure you can't include this information on the title page of the document itself?

2. Do you need to make comments that you don't want circulated with the primary document itself? For example, you may be submitting a proposal for installation of a specific computer feature and may need to make a statement such as, "I remember your comments when we talked June 2 about the difficulty you will have getting some of your operators to learn and use this feature; therefore, I have tried to simplify further the installation instructions." The recipient may want to circulate your proposal to his group but, of course, would be hesitant to do so with such a comment in the body of the proposal text. Such comments may be appropriate reason for a transmittal.

3. Do you need to make explanations or concessions that you don't want to include in the formal report or proposal itself? For example, you may propose to management that you can reduce production costs by changing vendors for a specific item and have all the figures worked out in the proposal. The only catch is that the product won't be available from the new vendor for another six months. In the transmittal you may want to explain that the due date, however, may be negotiable because your production people are now checking stock to see if they will need the item for the "interim" period. Or take another example: Perhaps in a proposal to a client you may want to mention a delivery date of May 30 for certain equipment. But in the transmittal, you may concede that if the buying decision turns on the client's having the equipment by May 20, you will do all within your power to go through nonroutine channels to get the shipment by the earlier date. Such concessions may be appropriate reason for a transmittal.

4. Do you need to provide an executive overview of the contents for readers who will not want to read the entire report or proposal?

Remember that most of the time, the overview should be included in the document being transmitted.

You'll notice that the recommendation at the beginning of this chapter doesn't say to eliminate all transmittals. If you have legitimate reason, write one. But take care that it accomplishes its purpose.

GUIDELINES FOR NECESSARY TRANSMITTALS

Mention the information you are transmitting first. This document, printout, check, invoice or report is the bottom-line message of interest. Ordinarily, in other letters and memos, you mention attachments or enclosures last.

List all enclosures specifically either in the body of the transmittal or after the "enclosure" notation at the bottom of the page. That may be the only way the recipient will know if something has been inadvertently omitted from a package of materials.

Include the reason for the information you're transmitting. Is it at the reader's request? For information only? To verify your own records? For processing? For approval? For distribution? Remember, however, that when you are sending information at the reader's request, you probably don't need to remind him or her. As a vice president at Tenneco recently commented to his managers, "If you send me another memo that says 'Pursuant to your request,' I'm going to wonder if you really think my memory is that bad." Finally, if the information being transmitted is routine, doesn't the recipient already know what it is and what to do with it?

Give a brief summary of the significant information contained in the attachment or enclosure. Depending on the document, this summary may mean only the amount of a check or invoice and its purpose or a lengthy paragraph about major findings contained in a complex computer printout. If you're transmitting a proposal to a customer or client, then your summary will be, in effect, your sales pitch—key benefits and costs.

Ask for the order and make it easy to respond. If the transmittal is going to a customer or client, don't assume he or she knows you want to make the sale. I've gotten proposals that sound perfunctory, as if I'd have to work really hard to get the sender's attention about the fact that I wanted to make a purchase. Consider enclosing some kind of response card to indicate further interest. At least give a business card and phone number.

Anticipate and answer possible questions about what you're transmitting. Are there unusual figures or facts that the reader may question? Are there omissions? If so, why? Will there be exceptions? If so, what are they? Providing the answers to these questions will save a follow-up call or memo explaining the first call or memo.

When appropriate, you may need to give your opinion about the enclosed or attached information. Do the enclosed sales figures indicate a trend, or do you think the slump is temporary due to some specific advertising disaster? Do you think the entire project will be completed by the proposed target date, or should you prepare the reader for the worst? In other words, prepare and/or interpret for the reader.

If you're not sending all the reader needs or has asked for, tell why not. Then let him or her know when to expect further information.

If, when you read the above guidelines, you have none of those reasons or tidbits of comment to make about information you're forwarding, then forget the formal transmittal memo or letter altogether and go to lunch early.

5
TO TRUST
OR TO
CONFIRM?

RECOMMENDATION: ELIMINATE HALF OF YOUR
CONFIRMATION LETTERS AND MEMOS. CREATE A
CLIMATE OF TRUST.

According to the Dartnell Institute of Research, which has been
keeping tabs on business writing for years, the average dictated letter
written in 1985 costs $8.52. If you must talk about confirming some-
thing complex such as a performance-appraisal promise, then that cost
rises for every minute you spend over the average of seven minutes for a
draft of a 185-190 word memo or letter.

But some will argue against eliminating ubiquitous confirmations,
saying you can't trust anybody anymore. In fact, it has become
commonplace among the savvy business professionals that written confirmations have taken the place of handshakes, that we need checks and
balances.

But that's not so in all organizations. Tom Peters in *A Passion for
Excellence* cites a speech made by a Dana Corporation executive vice
president: "We have no corporate procedures at Dana. We threw the
books away in the late sixties. We eliminated reports and sign-offs. We
installed trust."

In fact, many people pride themselves in doing business with and
working only for such organizations. I still deal with insurance agents
who say "you're covered" over the phone and have paid claims when

53

things still hadn't been put in writing. Writers have been dealing with literary agents for years without contracts guaranteeing their commissions on sales to publishers. Publishers and agents have been handshaking over the phone about agreed upon book and movie advances months before contracts have been drafted and signed. I, as well as others of my professional acquaintance, have distributed big-ticket items without having distribution agreements in writing. I've bought, sold, leased and "un-leased" real estate without having agreements in writing. And I don't think my experience is unusual.

That is not to say that I've never found others untrustworthy or have not discovered some people suffering from memory lapses! But here is where your ability to size people up comes into use. Most of us have a gut feeling about whom we can depend on and who will squirm in times of adversity.

QUESTIONS TO ASK BEFORE WRITING

Even when too much is at stake to rely on simple trust and even when your gut instinct tells you something should be put in writing, give it a second thought. Consider the following questions before committing things to paper.

Is Your Memory That Bad?

Is your memory so poor that you must record all the trivial details from interim conversations before final agreements are reached?

Some people are in the habit of recording every phone conversation and hall conversation for their files. And they may talk over a particular problem, situation or plan of action every day for a week before reaching a final agreement. Is your memory really that poor that you cannot recall what has been said in the last conversation? If it's important enough that you think you need to record it, chances are you'll remember it without the paperwork. And if any of these telephone conversations or details are going to be disputed, will your file record of your interpretation of the conversation make any difference?

Are You Going to Phone Anyway?

Are you going to call to follow up or to precede the paper confirmation?

So often that is the case with sales orders. A customer is in a hurry for the product; the salesperson turns in the order by phone and the merchandise is delivered before the paperwork is ever completed. If the phone call gets things done, why add the paperwork at all?

The same is true of many meetings and interviews. The attendees or interviewees are called to make sure there's no scheduling conflict, and then about two days after the meeting or interview the letter arrives confirming what's already taken place.

Or consider course announcements sent out by training directors. As people call to enroll in the class, the trainer records the names and confirms attendance on the phone. But just to make sure, several days before the class the trainer sends out a confirmation to all those who have already been confirmed on the phone. Then, one more time, to make sure there's no foul up and that all will show up for the class the next Monday morning, someone in Training once again phones all those confirmed. And those who somehow have forgotten the class or otherwise can't attend, drop out. In other words, the paper didn't hold them to their commitment anyway.

Ask yourself, what does the paper confirmation do that the phone call alone can't accomplish?

Will Confirmation Make Both Parties Feel Better about the Agreement?

If you sit down with the boss and discuss your past performance, your goals, your educational endeavors, and other experiences needed for advancement, will both of you feel better about having the discussion confirmed in writing? Possibly. But the boss may have justification in turning you down for a bonus or promotion if you haven't accomplished what you projected!

Or *you* may say "but you promised" if a particular reward isn't forthcoming. But will you? Will you actually go to the files and dig out the confirming memo and wave it in the boss's face? Will she agree that she is backing down on promises or simply state that when you wrote the confirming letter you misunderstood and did not record things quite as she remembers them?

For some, a written agreement is simply an attempt to protect a friendship, to think through a situation and to verify that you and another person have heard each other. If that's the case and neither of you trusts your oral communication and listening skills for accuracy, go ahead and commit to paper. But once you've thought it out, do you still need the paper? Three copies of it? In the files all year?

Will Confirmation Make Both Parties Feel Suspicious about the Agreement?

Have you noticed the basic resistance that surfaces when you've talked through a problem, a sale or contract and then get to signing the paperwork? In some people's minds, paper means "the fine print," "the catch," "the trap." In fact, nothing slows a sale down, creates doubt, and raises new questions like pushing paperwork at the customer or client.

Likewise, internally. Why do most people go for the paper, the rule book, the confirming memo? Not for directions. They go to the paperwork to find out whom they can blame for a foul-up. When you ask for a confirmation on internal matters, you're saying, "I want you signed on the dotted line to accept the rap." Does that imply confidence in the other's work or word?

What's the Worst That Can Happen If This Confirmation Is Not on Paper?

The owner of a thriving Houston barbecue restaurant has done away with his bills to customers. The waitresses simply tell the cooks the orders; when the customers leave the cashier asks, "What did you have?" and charges accordingly. The owner stands to lose his highest-priced menu item and stands to save the salary of an extra waitress or two and to gain customer goodwill.

The stakes, of course, get higher, much higher, in national and international business dealings. For Pennzoil, which had planned to merge with Getty Oil but had no signed contract, the stakes were $11.1 billion dollars (with interest). On November 19, 1985 a jury, nevertheless, found Texaco had unfairly upset the deal and awarded Pennzoil the largest civil damage award in U.S. history.

Although a written agreement may keep you out of court, before you write your confirmation, at least ask the question about what you have to lose and if the paperwork will prevent the loss.

Will the Confirmation Speed Up or Slow Down the Action?

On occasion, when the confirming memo or letter arrives on the reader's desk, it serves as a reminder that spurs him or her into action. But on other occasions, the reverse is true. What the other party may have agreed to on the phone may be postponed "just in case," when you say you'll be sending a confirmation in the mail. The person holds off on action just to be sure all details are correct on paper.

Organizations that promote intrapreneurial activities, in fact, find it essential to bypass the normal paperwork to get things done. Usually such groups have a senior executive who runs interference to get things done without following petty procedures and filling out forms.

If the *when* has anything to do with your particular situation, which effect do you intend—to speed up or to slow down the action?

If This Is Confirmed on Paper and the Other Party Tries to Back Out, What Measures *Could* You Take to Enforce the Agreement?

Will your confirmation cause the other party to go through with an agreement he or she is opposed to or has great incentive to violate? Is the confirmation a "gentlemen's" agreement anyway? Can you force a company to pay you or promote you as your confirmation memo states? Will the document stand up in court?

If This Is Confirmed on Paper and the Other Party Tries to Back Out, What Measures *Would* You Take to Enforce the Agreement?

A large oil company signed an agreement with a consulting petroleum engineer to develop a new piece of drilling equipment. The lucrative contract for the two-year project was suddenly canceled when a third-party marketing interest waned. The engineer found himself with a signed contract but no project. Although lawyers advised him to sue, he decided against it after asking himself the following questions: What do I hope to gain? Two years' salary. What do I have to lose? Two years' salary. The legal fees and no salary for the time spent in my lawyer's office and in court fighting the case. The goodwill of a large company for whom I plan to handle other projects when they arise. The potential business of other companies who may check references with this client.

There's a world of difference between *would* and *could*. Goodwill goes a long way. Before lengthy confirmations, don't leave it at *could you*, but instead ask, *would you*?

If after you've screened the situation with the seven previously given questions and still think a confirmation is in order, then follow these guidelines for making the one you write accomplish its purpose:

GUIDELINES FOR CONFIRMATIONS

Put the summary of what you are writing to confirm up front in the letter or memo. This confirmation is the bottom-line message of interest. Second, repeat all details of the situation: date, time, place, enclosures, amounts, qualifications, promises. In short, don't rely on any previous oral or written information; repetition of details is one of the main purposes of the written confirmation. Third, be sure to mention the date or manner of any initial phone, personal, or written contract/agreement/meeting/request. Fourth, unless obvious or routine, suggest how the recipient should contact you in case the confirmation note reveals some error or misunderstanding. Finally, provide signature lines for the reader/accepting officer.

If you continue to get follow-up questions about the confirmations you send and if you continue to change the details and working arrangements stated in the confirmation, take that as a good indication that the paper serves little purpose. You probably should be talking rather than writing.

6
REPORTS—THE
NECESSARY AND
THE UNNECESSARY

RECOMMENDATION: DO AWAY WITH UNNECESSARY
TRIP REPORTS, FIELD REPORTS, STATUS REPORTS, AND
ACTIVITY REPORTS THAT REDUCE PRODUCTIVITY OF
BOTH WRITER AND READER.

Despite all the grumbling I hear about paperwork in general and report writing in particular, surprisingly few employees (20 percent) consider their own reports unnecessary. Most label the ones they *receive* as unnecessary but not the ones they *write*. Obviously, professionals need guidance about what is and is not necessary to top-management readers. Senior executives at Marks and Spencer found this blind spot prevalent when they began wandering through the ranks, identifying unnecessary reports sent to top management.

With my own surveys, I've found that recognition of the unnecessary paperwork grows as employees rise in the company ranks: 9 percent of professionals with no supervisory responsibilities, 19 percent of middle managers, and 32 percent of senior managers say they are required to write unnecessary reports.

Therefore, the job of eliminating unnecessary reports falls to senior managers.

WHY BE LEERY ABOUT DASHING OFF A REPORT?

Costs

Studies within several organizations show the cost of generating reports ranges from $40 to $10,000, with the average cost being $500.

To figure the average cost of a business report in your company, ask the writers to tell you how many hours they spend putting together various reports. To get an accurate picture of the time involved, assure them that you are not checking up on them (which ensures that you get their "best" time) but that you actually want to see if the time is worth the effort. When you get the average number of hours for specific reports, plug into your formula the average report writer's salary to see how much that report costs each month. I have found the average report to be 2 1/4 pages long and to take 3 3/4 hours to compose. At a writer's salary of $35,000 that means the average report costs $65.62 to originate.

But that's only the beginning of the cost. You must also figure reading time for all those on the report's distribution list. Estimate how long it takes you to read the average report in your department, then plug an average hourly salary into the formula. Finally, multiply that reading time and cost by the number of people on the distribution list for the report.

Finally, multiply that cost for every such report written and read in your company. And remember that this figure does *not* include the clerical time for typing, filing, handling, retrieval, or storage of the report.

Writing and reading reports is expensive.

But, cost aside, there are other reasons for eliminating unnecessary reports.

Many Go Unread

Computers spew out reams of unnecessary, useless, uninterpreted and untargeted printouts. Most go unread until someone comes along and interprets the information into action or inaction.

Other reports that do contain interpreted and summarized information go unread simply because they contain much more than the reader wants to know on the subject. Very few senior managers read reports in their entirety, instead depending on the Overview, Conclusions, and Recommendations sections to give them all the information they need.

A staff analyst at a large oil company insists (along with many other professionals preparing reports) that it's not top managers but middle and lower-level managers who demand the lengthy reports. And I agree. He explains:

> "Take my job. I work on long research projects, gathering information and then presenting it to top management. And I never know how much to write in the report to accompany my talk. It's *my* feeling that I should write a report that covers the highlights, not every single detail. Of course, I'll have all the good stuff, so to speak, at my fingertips. And if they want to know how or why I came up with a particular figure, I can tell them. But my *boss* says, 'No, write it all down in the report.' So I do. And we distribute copies at the meetings. The big guys come in, listen, talk it over, and make a decision. And they walk out, leaving all those report copies—all those details—lying on the table. The long report was really written for my boss."

That is not to say that the research or fact gathering is unnecessary. The act of actually writing a formal report, however, is often the unnecessary step.

Many Contain Information Given Orally

Many field reports, trip reports and activity reports contain information phoned in to the boss during or immediately after the situation developed or the trip was made. The written reports serve only to provide a rehash of the oral reports. Then they go into the files, never to be retrieved.

Consider the case of the external consultant. How many times does the client ask for a final report from the consultant (or the consultant offers it unasked) when the consultant has already given the client all the information face to face or on the phone? If you've been given the information already, why demand it again in writing?

As an engineering consultant explained: "If I didn't have to write the reports, I could spend a lot more time in the field gathering information. And basically, when I finish a job, I immediately phone the client and tell him what I found out. But if he wants a report, I write the report ... and bill for the time it takes to write it."

Do you really want to pay for three hours of the consultant's time when he/she can give you the same information face to face in 15 minutes?

I'm not saying that consultants never need to write reports on their work. Simply question the automatic procedure, case by case.

Many Contain Information Already Available in Other Formats

Forty-three percent of the survey respondents who said they were required to write unnecessary reports mentioned reports containing information already available in other formats. Such reports were the single most frequently cited creators of unnecessary paperwork.

A retired sales manager related what he considered a humorous awareness of such duplication:

> "The data-processing department put out a report in a certain format and sent it down the hall to the vice president. He said he couldn't use it in that format, so he had his secretary reformat the whole thing. I saw the secretary redoing it one day and asked her why. Her explanation was, 'Because he told me to.' So I finally just butted in and asked the VP if he didn't know that the DP department could have sent him the information directly in the correct format the first time around. He never thought of that."

A petroleum engineer explained the gathering and reformatting process in his department:

> "My manager has the three engineers who report to him prepare progress reports. Then he puts them all together—just takes various sections of ours—and summarizes them in another report to the coordinator. Then the coordinator gets these reports from the managers. He, then, condenses and extracts from the managers' reports and prepares a report to the vice president. Then the vice president extracts what he wants and puts it in his report to the board. I don't see why we couldn't just cut out about two layers here."

They probably should.

They Reduce Time Available for More Productive Pursuits

For the salesperson, time spent on paperwork means less time for sales. A 1982 Booz, Allen, & Hamilton study involving nearly 300 knowledge workers, who recorded 90,000 time samples over 3,700 workdays, found that salespeople spent only 36 percent of their time prospecting and selling!

To the field engineer, report writing is time away from inspections, troubleshooting, or whatever. An engineer at an oil service company recently lamented, "I'm so far behind with my reports, you wouldn't believe it. I have 157 reports to get out." He couldn't bring himself to halt his work to do the paperwork. But you can be sure that the companies they were servicing were still operating; the lack of a written report didn't slow up their progress in resolving the problems the engineer/inspector had discovered. The after-the-fact report writing only served to give the involved engineer an energy-sapping, time-wasting morale damper.

To all those in service industries such as banks, brokerage houses and consulting firms, time spent on paper is time away from customers and profits.

Professional and specialty journals are rife with testimonials from various organizations large and small about increased productivity after eliminating daily and weekly activity reports.

They Cover Up for Lack of Meaningful Results

Many employees write reports to cover up a lack of anything to say. They may even try to cover up for bad news or threatening trends that might be more difficult to downplay in a face-to-face confrontation.

External reports are often written for the same reasons. In a meeting with engineering consultants who wanted help in setting up their report formats, I had been suggesting a bulleted format with informative headings to help the client/reader quickly focus on important findings. This was the conversation that followed among the group of engineers, field people, and the vice president of operations:

First engineer: You know, I understand what you're saying. In fact, I think this whole report we're looking at could be cut in half if we bullet the key findings and work performed.

Field inspector: Yeah, why do we write all this stuff in long sentences and paragraphs? We just say the same things in several different ways.

Second engineer: Sure would be a lot quicker to get reports out.

Third engineer: But wait a minute. The reason we use this report and add all this padding is so the client'll think he's getting his money's worth. Basically, we have the same procedures we go through on every job. But if we're up front about what we do and if we do several jobs for one client, things would look too cut-and-dried.

Vice president: Right. That's been our rationale. So let's ... let's keep this paragraph format and go on from here. If we told them in plain English what we did, why would they need us?

I once asked a geologist if he had a typical geological report that he could let me read just to acquaint myself with the nature of technical reports coming from his department. He swiveled around to his credenza, retrieved a nine-page report and tossed it in my lap. "Try this. It takes nine pages there to say that if you want to dig more coal, you need a bigger shovel."

I laughed, but after reading the impressively titled report and after wading through graphs, charts and columns of figures, I decided his summary was quite accurate. If you have nothing to say, a report is a good way to say it.

Many Are Requested But Few Wanted

Some managers ask for reports much as personnel directors say "send me a résumé" when they're not hiring, or customers say "that sounds interesting" when they're not buying.

A data-processing specialist, having a great deal of difficulty putting together a lengthy report to his boss, asked me for help. My first question, of course, was: Why did the boss want the report? After hemming and hawing through several explanations, he finally came up with this: "Well, you see, what we're really doing is taking over—or attempting to take over—some of the support problems of data processing in our area because DP doesn't have the time or the manpower to help us with our peculiar situations. So the boss asked me to write this report to tell him how we would take over the project and oversee support for the whole division on data-processing questions."

"Okay," I interrupted, "how much of this information does your boss already know?"

Oh, I already told him everything we plan to do," he assured me. "Actually, I don't really know why he wants the report *now*. I think he just wants the massive details to see how much command we have of what the project involves."

The next time someone requests a report from you or your department, do a little probing—or a lot of probing. The requester's vague, "Why don't you put something together on that for me?" can mean several things:

1. You don't look busy; here's something for you to do.
2. I've got to have something to show *my* boss to prove that we're doing something over here.
3. Leave me alone; I'm interested in something else now.
4. I don't know enough about what you're trying to tell me to discuss it with you; educate me and then I'll let you know if it's worth pursuing.
5. You're on to a good idea (or meaningful information); I'd like to follow that up.

You'll save both your time and the boss's if you act only when the interpretation is number 4 or 5 above.

HOW TO DETERMINE IF A REPORT IS NECESSARY

Can You Get the Right Answers from the One Who Asked for the Report?

If one of the vague requests mentioned above comes from the boss, ask questions to determine what he or she really means. Ask for a conference and proceed to ask the questions any boss should be ready to answer:

- Who is the audience?
- Why am I writing the report?
- What special problems should I be aware of in gathering and presenting the information?

- What background do I need?
- Who and what are my resources?

If you can get appropriate answers to these questions, then consider the request for a report a serious one and proceed. If you can't, drag your feet.

Is the Report Essential for the Work to Get Done?

In other words, if you were delayed for two weeks by illness in your preparation of the report, would someone waiting on your report hold up the project or the decision? Or is your report just a document to the file explaining what action has already been taken or why decisions have already been made in case something goes wrong and someone needs protection?

Can You Find the Same Information Already Compiled Elsewhere?

Information does not necessarily mean paper. And, more important, information doesn't have to be contained in house to be valid and useful for your organization's function. Can you buy on-line time to a database that can provide all you need to know? If the information you need is specialized and should be originated within the organization, check to see if it is. Researchers continually report that companies spend money each year duplicating research simply because abstracts are so poorly written that nobody knows what's already been done, gathered, and reported.

Perhaps your first place to look is on the forms scattered around the company and in the reams of printouts. Your report may simply be a new format for already available information.

Or, as the engineer quoted earlier observed, maybe you can cut out two or three layers of report extracting, condensing, and rewriting. Why not skip several layers and have a coordinator at the top do all the extracting and condensing and compile one report to go directly to the vice president?

Does the End Justify the Means?

Is the requester of the report aware of the amount of time the report will require? Often a boss has the idea that such-and-such report could be put together in a couple of days, when in reality the report requires two weeks. If the requester of the report knew the effort involved, would the results of the report justify that labor cost?

A freelance publicist friend of mine was asked to put together a very specialized media kit for a newly targeted women's market. She quoted the daily fee to the manager of the project who okayed the work. But when the publicist came back two weeks later with the media kit and the bill, the project manager froze at her desk when she heard the price. It took her a full two minutes to stand, turn her back to gaze out the window, and compose herself enough to ask why so much time was involved.

Needless to say, the cost of gathering the facts for developing the kit far exceeded the advertising dollars she'd hoped to generate with the small new market. The tendency is to point a wiser-than-thou finger at the project manager for not asking for an estimate of the total time involved. After all, who would be so foolish as to deal with an outside firm without an estimate or a firm bid?

Yet managers seldom apply the same wisdom to internal reports. Is the cost of the preparation time and the loss of more productive time for other pursuits worth the results you hope to gain from the report?

Will the Report Be Outdated Before It's Completed?

Conditions change. Frequently projects for which reports were assigned to pave the way have been completed before the report! Does the client seem as interested in the proposal as when you first talked and assigned the report to a subordinate? Are there rumors that top management has already made a decision based on unexpected events since the report was requested?

Time-management experts suggest that one way to find more time is to stall in the event that the writing project may become unnecessary altogether.

HOW TO ELIMINATE THE UNNECESSARY

But what about all the unnecessary reports that are already routine—how do you begin to eliminate these?

Wean the Reader Gradually

Wean the reader by gradually lengthening the reporting time. If you report every week, ask why not every *other* week? If you report monthly, ask if you can make it quarterly. Then, after you've cut frequency, start condensing. If you usually send the report in the MADE format (see Chapter 7), at first you'll include the bottom-line message or overview, then the next action you plan to take or what action you're recommending the reader take, and then the details. Finally, you'll supply attachments as further optional evidence.

Gradually your report will come to consist only of an overview message, recommendations and few supporting details. The ideal will be to end up with reports that include only the bottom-line message and the recommendations or request for approval on your next action. If the reader wants supporting details, he or she can ask.

Consider "Exception" Reporting and Make Sure You Define the Exception

Why should you spend time writing—and the manager spend time reading—reports that say the same thing over and over every week or every month. A marketing representative claims that she spends six hours a week putting together a weekly management report, which she then summarizes into a monthly report. "How does the monthly report differ from the other weekly reports?" I asked.

"Oh, it's just a repeat of what I've already submitted each week. I just put them all together."

Then her colleague across the lunch table asked, "Where do you get the information for your reports?"

"From those reports you send me."

"Good, I'm glad somebody uses those things. I never have known why I was submitting that information or who got it."

"Oh, the same information is available in several reports," the marketing rep responded. "I guess they just want to look at it in different forms."

When you find yourself reporting the same information week to week or month to month, consider reporting—or having your staff report—only the exceptions. Does this customer need special attention? Have we had a sharp increase in complaints about a certain product? Have sales risen drastically? Dropped drastically? Has a specific advertising campaign spurred unusual demand? Is a certain project lagging behind schedule, and do you need to take precautions to minimize effects on other areas? Do you have a new product idea gleaned from a customer? Do you have an outstanding lead you plan to follow up next week?

With "exception" reporting, you have something meaningful to say, and your messages usually get attention.

If you're the boss who has adopted the exception reporting idea, make sure your staff understands the concept. A district manager of a public utility company, who reports directly to a vice president, recently said to me: "We use the 'exception' reporting idea around here. On our progress reports each month, my boss doesn't want us to tell him about the routine things; he only wants us to tell him the unusual. You know, some months I really have to do some thinking to find something to write him about."

Here's an "exception" report he sent to the boss.

Subject: North Coast Division Activity

The workload has remained comparable with previous months. We have not seen the influx of what used to be relocating prior to schools opening. Viewing the economy from this angle indicates only a stable or minimal growth.

I have received a list of candidates for the service supervisor's job, and we are interviewing them at this time.

Don't assume that your employees understand the concept of exception reporting. In fact, you may have to assure them that it's okay not to write *at all* if they have nothing more to say than "we're getting along fine."

Threaten to Stop Sending the Report

Try attaching a cover memo that says, "To cut down on distribution costs and to reduce your reading load, I plan to stop sending this report unless I hear from you." Then if you don't hear, stop sending it. You may find that no one asks you to keep sending the report.

Or, when readers reply that they do indeed want to keep receiving your report, ask why they need it. If they have a legitimate reason, then perhaps you can locate another report that's already being prepared containing the same information. Substitute that report and stop sending the one you prepare. If you force your readers to actually read and respond to some of the long reports you send, they may decide it's not worth the trouble to read them.

When readers do respond that they have a need to know, ask if the report meets—or more than meets—their objectives. Is it timely? Is there a format that would be more useful? How about the details—are they necessary? (Suggest a shorter format that gives the same big-picture message and you'll usually better meet the needs of the management reader.)

Use Alternatives Such As Visuals

If you decide that the information you have does need to be sent, look for alternate ways to present it, ways that do not require as much writing and reading and paper in general.

Can you prepare visuals and give the same information in a more meaningful way, facilitating feedback and action more quickly?

George Blake, vice president at Anderson, Clayton & Company, S.A., writing in the *Harvard Business Review* (March-April 1978) says his company has scrapped longer reports, particularly those with long tables of figures, in favor of about 20 or so mini charts on one page. The page resembles a balance sheet that shows monthly sales, profits, common stock, receivables, inventory, market share, interest rates, cash flow, etc. The one-page visual format allows the audience to get the big picture much more readily than with 10 pages of words. The one-page visual is also ideal for meeting presentations and for travel.

Encourage "Management By Wandering Around"

Peters and Waterman, in their bestseller, *In Search of Excellence*, first coined the phrase "management by wandering around." You may decide as manager that you prefer to wander around to see what your staff is doing rather than to read their reports and interpretations of what's going on. Being with people rather than pushing paper puts you in a better position to motivate, to understand real difficulties as they develop on the job, and to keep close to the product, service and customer.

Erroneously, managers often consider such observation as "soft" data as opposed to "hard" data (read computer printout). Actually, both kinds of data can be soft or hard. Statistics do lie.

Build Trust by Being Thorough

When you've passed all the report screening questions, learned all the whys of what you write and eliminated all the unnecessary paperwork, then use the extra time to prepare the necessary reports thoroughly and correctly.

When you send few, well-done and meaningful reports, people read them. They trust that you have something to say and that you've said it well.

How to be thorough? First, check numbers, dates, figures. When there's an error, you lose credibility and maybe much more. Learn where errors tend to creep into the kinds of reports you write and always double-check those points. For example, computer support centers gradually learn that their users call in with similar problems. They keep records of those calls and gradually have a "routine" checklist to correct problems. Likewise, after a while you know where the errors in your reports occur and where readers will have questions. Anticipate and answer those questions or objections the first time around.

Second, delegate the writing assignment to your most knowledgeable person—not the one who happens to be relatively free for a day or two. As I mentioned in Chapter 2, the most frequent cause of the edit/rewrite/ edit/rewrite syndrome is delegating the writing to the person with the lowest level of knowledge about the whole situation.

Finally, keep up to date. Don't report yesterday's problems or information. Make sure your report covers the most current questions, trends, and concerns of your reader. Week-old reports aren't any more useful than week-old newspapers.

Instill this same commitment to thoroughness and correctness in your employees. When you hear from them, let them know you want to hear something meaningful—NBA (no busywork accepted).

7
CONCISENESS

RECOMMENDATION: ADOPT THE NEED-TO-KNOW,
"MADE" FORMAT COMPANYWIDE TO KEEP
DOCUMENTS SHORT AND TO ENCOURAGE READERS TO
STOP READING AS SOON AS THEY HAVE THE NECESSARY
INFORMATION.

Today's corollary to the frontier's "Go west, young man, go west" is "Be brief, young man, be brief." To the best of my recollection, I've never conducted a workshop where someone did not ask, "What do you think of the one-page memo?"

In other words, the message is out. But some haven't bought it. A long-time corporate lawyer analyzed his company this way: "Top management says, 'Be brief.' But it's middle management that wants all the paperwork. In case they get called on the carpet, they want something to show."

And if most managers do believe in brevity, many still may not understand the why or know the how of it. For example, a technical curriculum designer for one of the largest computer companies in the nation explained that each of their instruction manuals are filled with between one hundred and two hundred pages of unnecessary, duplicated information. "We have the same old comments, 'Check the equipment before time for the presentation,' 'Make sure you have spare bulbs for the projector,' etc. over and over in every manual we write. The instructors have to wade through pages and pages before getting to anything new."

"How could you improve the manual design then?" I asked.

"We should publish a standard teaching guide with all the general information. Then each specific curriculum guide would have to be only a few pages rather than hundreds."

"Then why don't you?" I persisted.

"That's just the way they want it."

I didn't follow up about who "they" were with this fourteen-year employee and veteran curriculum writer, but you get the picture.

Others *do* know the why of their verbosity and paperwork. A banking consultant explained that his firm has two formats for reports to clients, format A and format B. "When we accomplish a lot, we just get right to the point and tell them our recommendations right up front. When we don't find out much we add a lot of background, go into our methodology section—a little of everything before we get to the conclusions at the end."

The result of unnecessary paperwork is the same: Companies and their employees suffer regardless of whether the unnecessary is "innocently" inflicted because of ignorance about how to curb it or is inflicted as an attempt at deception.

The why and the how of brevity—those two issues need attention in the rest of the chapter.

WHY BE CONCISE?

Reading Is Expensive

According to my survey responses, employees spend the following amounts of their time each week reading job-related materials (to check the accuracy of these estimates, we put the question to them in two ways: percentage of time spent on reading paperwork coming to their desks and hours per week spent reading job-related materials):

senior managers	25 percent	16 hours
middle managers	23 percent	13 hours
professionals with no supervisory responsibilities	18 percent	10 hours

*The hours and percentages were not limited to a 40-hour work week.

As you can see, the figures rise slightly according to the rank of the reader. These hours are the equivalent of the time it would take to read two or three novels on the job every week. That's why senior executives put conciseness on the top of the list of objectives for business writing training.

Fill in a representative annual salary, plus benefits, for employees in each category above and then multiply that figure by the number on your payroll per category to get some idea of how much your company spends on reading the paperwork you shuffle.

Obviously, you can't eliminate reading costs completely. But you can reduce them significantly by adopting a format that mandates shorter, layered documents. Layering documents simply means writing them so that the usual three layers of readers in your organization—decision makers, professionals reading to be updated, and technical specialists—can read as much or as little as they need to do their job. (You'll see "layered" models later in the chapter.)

Consider the Customer's Frame of Mind

A second reason, in addition to reading costs, for keeping documents short is that excessive paperwork scares clients and customers. If you tell your customers or clients in a few moments about your service or your product and then hand them a long proposal, they often get scared of the fine print. Perhaps, their reasoning follows, the length contains "the catch" you didn't mention.

What's more, your customers don't want to have to work too hard to deal with you. If you force them to read through a two-page sales letter, a couple of brochures, and a six-page proposal, they may just decide it's not worth the effort to find out what you have to say. Especially if the competitor can say it more quickly and clearly. Remember that TV commercials run only 30-60 seconds. Why should you think customers' attention spans are so much greater when you give them the message on paper?

Even more important, having the customer read the fine print may be to your best advantage. Nothing irritates customers and lowers their inclination to deal with you more than to find out later that they've signed something they never intended to agree to. Even though you gave them the facts in your memo, letter, report, or proposal, usually they tend to blame you for manipulating them and hiding things in the gobbledygook.

Everything I've just said about dealing with clients or customers applies equally to those you have to "sell" within your organization—whether a peer on cooperation or a boss on an increase in your budget.

Brevity Reduces the Chance for Error

Reader aside, what's in it for you, the writer, to be brief?

Well, the longer the document, the more likely the chance of grammatical or clarity errors that destroy your credibility. A purchasing agent for a large oil company brought me a proposal from someone trying to sell him drilling equipment. The proposal had the word "indispensable" misspelled. The buyer went on to explain why his company had quit purchasing from that manufacturer: "If they can't even spell correctly when they describe their equipment, how do we know their technology is any better?"

Unusual? Maybe. But not rare. I have a cache of such stories from people I work with in different organizations.

Aside from increasing your opportunity to damage your credibility, verbosity often forces you to spend time interpreting and following up. Although some writers send out "boilerplate" proposals to clients or reports to top management to save time, they often wind up spending more time on answering questions about how the boilerplate paragraph "doesn't actually apply in this case." (If you use a boilerplate document, at least cut out the nonapplicable parts for each use.)

You Can Spend More Productive Time Elsewhere

And finally to your advantage in reducing the length and increasing the clarity of your documents, you have more time to spend on selling, consulting, decision-making, buying, policy setting or whatever else you do to contribute to the profit margin.

However, verbosity is a difficult habit to break, for several reasons. In school we were given assignments by length. Even in college the professors were still saying, "I don't think you'll be able to cover the subject in fewer than 10 pages."

Insecurities are another reason writers ramble on rather than get to the point. Employees are not always sure how much the reader trusts their data and reasoning; therefore, they add copious details on every point, no matter how minor. And if the information is inaccurate, incomplete, or questionable, the long-winded writer can always hope that the boss grades on effort. After all, paperwork represents work, doesn't it?

It's not easy to be concise. Pascal wrote, "I have made this letter longer than usual, because I lack the time to make it short." It may take a writer longer to write a four-paragraph memo and say what's important than to write an eight-paragraph memo in "once-upon-a-time" form that forces the reader to figure out the meaning and the action the communication calls for. Brevity doesn't come easily for most. Thomas Jefferson observed, "The most valuable of all talents is never using two words when one word will do."

Remember That Less Is Usually More

You may help your reader comprehend much more by writing much less. Obviously, that's true in speaking. Experienced speakers choose one theme and about three key points and then keep hammering away at them, hoping that the less there is to retain, the more the audience will focus on the primary issues.

The same is true in paperwork. Less usually means more—more understanding, more focus, more clarity, more action, more time saved.

An employee at one of the nation's largest corporations recently won $18,000 in his company's incentive-awards program for an idea he submitted—on a single page. Originally, he had taken 19 pages to address the complex subject and its implications. But, following the advice of both his first-level and second-level managers, he worked to condense the idea to one page. Upon presentation of the award check, the vice president commented that the award committee was particularly impressed that he was able to express such a complex idea with such brevity. The vice president explained that if the submission had been longer, they unfortunately would probably not have read it and would have missed an excellent idea.

Realize that your superiors have perhaps a dozen reports of about the same length as yours coming to their desks every day for review or action. Make a judgment about how much they need to know. (Questions listed below will help you to make that judgment.) The reader can't tell you how much you need to write until he or she is familiar with your subject. And if that were the case, you probably wouldn't need to prepare the report at all. You, the writer, are in the better position to decide the appropriate length of what you write. Go for brevity.

So much for the "whys" of short documents—costs, customer acceptance, clarity, productivity. Let's get to the hows.

Make Sure What You Write Is Readable

Don't "implement complexity" into your work (as one engineer confided that he did). The old "golly gee, will this ever impress 'em" report rarely does. Dump the jargon and unnecessary A to Z explanations that make you sound as though you don't know how to tailor a message to your audience.

The mark of a good motivational speaker is an ability to meet the audience on common ground. Although most platform speakers who address groups all over the country—whether corporations, churches, professional organizations, or family seminars—have only five or six speeches, they know that tailoring the message to the audience is the key to success.

When you try to "tell 'em everything you know," you often obscure what *they* want to know. When you're new in the organization, the only way you have to write is up; therefore, a common concern is to impress. Most people translate that to mean length. Only when you get to the higher ranks in the company do you have the confidence and the good sense to understand the necessity of being direct.

USE THE *MADE* FORMAT

Basically, the MADE format is a variation of the journalistic inverted pyramid. In the business world, we have the same kind of writers and readers as newspapers have across the nation. Business writers, as well as newspaper writers, are writing to *express* rather than to *impress*. Likewise, business readers, as well as newspaper readers, want the information as quickly as possible so they can get on to other things. They are reading to be informed, not entertained.

You may recognize another similarity in the MADE format detailed below. The Marine Corps teaches its officers the five-paragraph format:

Situation: Where are we and where is the enemy?
Mission: What is the objective?
Execution: What are we going to do?

Administration: How will we resupply?

Command and control: What's the signal?

Therefore, since on most occasions business writers and readers have the same purposes, they should not spend valuable time reinventing the format every time they send out a memo, letter, report, or proposal.

For this reason, I suggest the MADE format (or a variation) be adopted companywide for 90 percent of all documents. (There are a few exceptions—direct-mail sales letters, "negative" responses, and some others that I won't go into in this book but that are addressed in my other books, *Would You Put That in Writing?* and *Send Me a Memo.*) Writers can simply plug their new message into the MADE format, avoiding wasted time on several drafts prepared in their process of finding out what they want to say.

Let me explain the MADE format and then give the reasons behind it.

M: *Message*—What is the big-picture, bottom-line message of inter-est to your reader(s)?

A: *Action*—What action do you plan to take next based on this message? Or what action do you want your reader to take based on this message? (Not all your memos, letters and reports will call for action or make recommendations. If they do, however, here in this second section is where those actions belong.)

D: *Details*—Who, when, where, why, how, how much? Not all details should be included in every communication, of course. In-clude only those that are necessary—usually the *why* and *how* details. On many occasions, those details that can be answered in only one word or a short phrase will already be stated in the first or second opening "message" sentences. But if one of those details needs elaboration, here in this third section is where that elabora-tion goes.

E: Optional *Evidence*—Mention the attachments or enclosures you're sending along to make the message clearer or the action easier to take. Tables. Charts. Graphs. Copies of past correspondence. In-correct invoices. Last year's contract with disputed areas highlighted for discussion. Et cetera.

To illustrate the above MADE format, examine the following four pairs of memos. The first of each pair follows the traditional once-upon-a-time format; the second, the functional MADE format.

Memo 1
Traditional Format

Subject: Lease Security Policy

Attached for your information is the company's recently drafted lease security policy. The policy is self-explanatory; however, if you have any questions or require any clarification, please give me a call.

I am particularly interested in the status of each of our regions in regard to locking all oil and water storage-tank valves because this matter was noted by the AG auditors as a deficiency during their reviews. Could you please inform me of the status of your region in relationship to this objective by August 15? Please include a list of all deficient lease sites (if any) with your response and note your plans for securing those sites.

Thanks for your cooperation on this matter.

Sincerely,

MADE Format

Subject: Audit Report—Lease Security Policy

The AG auditors have noted a deficiency in the locking of all oil and water storage-tank valves at the various regions.

Could you please evaluate this situation in your region and give me your results by August 15? In your report, please include a list of all deficient lease sites and your plans for securing those sites.

Attached for your information is the company's recently drafted lease security policy.

Sincerely,

Memo 2
Traditional Format

Subject: Overton Survey Results and Recommendation to Forego
Installation

Wednesday, June 15, John Smith and I met Bill McDonald in
Littleton to survey the Overton area on Lake Littleton west of the
town of Littleton. Overton is on the shore of Lake Littleton
between the Twin River and Winapoo Creek. Highway 90 runs
through the town.

*Once-
upon-
a-time-
details*

We drove out Highway 90 from Littleton to Overton, measuring
approximately 14 miles from the Highway 39 bypass to the west
side of Winapoo crossing. We rode through town to the Twin
River bridge and drove through some of the residential areas both
north and south of Highway 90. Highway 90 is commercial, con-
sisting mostly of very small strip centers and single offices with
quite a bit of undeveloped property. The old section of Overton
consists of small wood-frame houses on large lots. The newer
residential "pockets" are also generally small houses and generally either frame construction or mobile homes. Within a developed
"pocket," the houses are on small lots, but there are vacant lots
scattered throughout the "pockets." Also there is usually quite a
distance between these "pockets" of development.

There is quite a bit of lot-sales activity in the area. This activity
ranges from gravel roads cut out through the woods with mobile
home lots on either side to paved streets fronted by home sites for
sale. There are only a few houses being constructed. Potential land
sales could be several thousand lots. All this activity is taking
place in an 8-10 square mile area (roughly four miles long by two
miles wide). Several hundred homes have been built in the last
five to seven years. Mr. Sanders supposedly counted 1,550 houses
in the area he proposes to serve. We did not attempt to make a
house count, but we seriously doubt there are 1,550 houses in the
area. The local propane dealer in Littleton says he has about 900
propane customers scattered over the north and east side of Lake
Littleton. Even if there are 1,550 houses in the area, the 900
butane customers are the only ones that could reasonably be expected to connect to natural gas if a system were installed.

*details-
suspense
builds!*

Using 20 miles of high pressure four-inch feed line, 20 miles of two-inch intermediate pressure main and 900 customers at 50 Mcf each per year, we estimate a cost of $1,300,000 to install Mr. Sanders' proposed distribution system. This installation would require rates of approximately $9.65/Mcf to make the system economically feasible. This price is equivalent to propane at 90 cents per gallon, with propane now selling at or below 90 cents. This rate would make wholesale conversion of propane customers unlikely. Attached is a cost analysis and economic data.

suspense builds!

optional evidence

The Overton area is sparsely developed, the number of existing potential customers is small, and future development is unpredictable. The economics of extending a distribution system to the area is poor due to lack of customers and high rates that would be necessary to show a return.

message buried here

MADE Format

Subject: Overton Survey Results and Recommendation to Forego Installation

After our June 15 survey of the Overton area, we find that the area is sparsely developed, the number of existing potential customers is small, and future development is unpredictable. The economics of extending a distribution system to the area is unfavorable; therefore, the survey team recommends that we not install lines at this time.

message

action

Using 20 miles of high pressure four-inch feed lines, 20 miles of two-inch intermediate pressure main and 900 customers at 50 Mcf each per year, we estimate a cost of $1,300,000 to install Mr. Sanders' proposed distribution system. Installation would require rates of approximately $9.65/Mcf to make the system economically feasible. This price is equivalent to propane at 90 cents per gallon, with propane now selling at or below 90 cents. This rate would make wholesale conversion of propane customers unlikely.

important details

Attached is a cost analysis and economic data.

Memo 3
Traditional Format

Subject: Rating Given XYZ Customer

The customer called the center only once. The caller did not adequately state his environment; therefore, he did not get enough information. Joe Miller, who placed the call, replied to the survey. Joe called the center and asked how to create user panels with DSEF. Al Horn took the call and answered the question. The customer was not knowledgeable on the product. At the time of the call, the customer was having problems using, evoking and understanding DSEF, but did not ask any questions about these issues. The specialist had no knowledge of this. The specialist discussed ways to accomplish the task with DSEF-ITN. Joe thinks that ITN is only available in the ITN/NOP environment. Thus, the caller did not understand the supplied answer nor believe it, thus prompting the statement: "Could be more knowledgeable about software products as they relate to XYZ as opposed to NOP."

details that make no sense yet

part of the message

The customer perceives his rating to be favorable and did not have any recommendations for improvements.

I discussed the survey with Art Boyle, and he was able to shed light on the customer situation. Art said the customer had been trying to create user panes in DSEF. He said they had been given conflicting information—both that it could and could not be done.

more details

He'd entered SAME questions and had gotten conflicting answers. They finally received help from DSEF Development. He felt the customer had not used our center enough, but they were experienced in XYZ. He felt the customer would look favorably on a follow-up call.

rest of the message

Because the customer still thinks ITN is not available in the XYZ environment, a follow-up courtesy marketing call with the SE and the customer may be appropriate.

action

MADE Format

Subject: Rating Given XYZ Customer

I have researched the customer-service rating on XYZ customer and found that the customer, Joe Miller, did not intend his comment on the customer-service survey to be negative. Because of his lack of product knowledge, he thought that he had received varying answers on the same questions. But after our discussion, he concluded that he was simply not knowledgeable enough about the DSEF product and had not made enough use of our support service to get help with his problem.

message

Since the customer still does not think the ITN is available in the XYZ environment, I think a follow-up call by Marketing and the SE is appropriate.

action

Memo #4
Traditional Format

Subject: Performance Summary of Max Perkins

The following summarizes performance background, ratings, merit increases, performance discussions, and documentation of subject employee.

Max Perkins was employed on November 2, 198– and was subsequently transferred from Production to Headquarters Administration on July 10, 198–. At the time of transfer to the Material Control function, John Adams indicated that a problem existed between Max and Fred Boston, Max's supervisor. He was not sure of the cause of the problem but felt that I should be aware that the situation existed.

I reviewed the rejected-tubulars claims status with Max and Fred Boston in August 198– and was shocked to find out that we had about $3.5 million in backlog of claims. Fred indicated that Max had not handled the job on a current basis. Max blamed the situation on his predecessor and the accounting department. At this point I asked them to give me a status report each month so that I could monitor the progress. In early September 198–, I realized that the function needed to be moved to the Procurement group in order to use our leverage with the suppliers and mills in getting reimbursement for rejected materials purchased by our division. I told Max I was really disappointed with his performance and his allowing this situation to develop. Max's reaction was that he didn't feel responsible, didn't like the detail involved, and thought the job he was hired to do was misrepresented to him. About one month later Max came to me, expressing a desire to work in some other part of the organization, and I explained that he needed to improve his performance in his present assignment before I would recommend him for transfer.

details
once-upon-a-time arrangement

In October 198–, I assigned Bob Frison, a purchasing analyst, to the claims function previously handled by Max. Within five months the claims outstanding dropped from $3.5 million to about $0.5 million.

In February 198–, the function was assigned to Mark Wright, another purchasing analyst, who continued Frison's progress and held the claims within a range of $200,000 to $500,000.

details – Suspense builds!

Max's performance continued to be average or below average for the next few months due to his obvious disinterest in his job assignment.

Max had been rated a 2.5 in Production, but his rating dropped to a 3.0 in the last two review periods due to his poor performance.

In November 198–, we decided to move Max from Material Control to Procurement. Since the claims were in excellent shape, we wanted to give Max another chance under a different supervisor (Attachment 1). We explained to Max that his merit increase was being delayed due to his poor performance. (See note on the approved merit salary sheet, Attachment 2.) After two months his performance was reviewed and a merit increase approved. (See memos in file from Ted Howard, Manager, Procurement, Attachment 3.)

optional evidence

optional evidence

optional evidence

In July 198–, we made some internal moves because of the problems encountered with the claims situation again. (See memos from Mark Wright on the status report, dated August 20, 198–, Attachment 4, and Dick Robert's memo on Max's performance, dated August 1, 198–, Attachment 5.)

optional evidence

On November 29, 198–, I called Max in and reviewed his history of performance. He stated he "knew it wasn't good, but he didn't think it was that bad" (Attachment 6). I reviewed the memo from Fred Boston (Attachment 7), dated October 10, 198–, with him, and he said, "I thought I was pleasing Mr. Boston now." Max asked if he could be transferred. He felt that he would like to be in Planning XYZ, Inc. I explained that I didn't transfer poor performers and that his performance didn't merit a move. We had discussed this same subject on a previous occasion. I asked Max to visit Fred, and at this point I called Tim Black from Employee Relations to visit with me about Max's performance and to get his opinions on releasing Max.

more details

Tim reviewed the file and then asked to visit with Max about his performance. Tim found that Max was not interested in his work and wanted an opportunity to transfer to another department within XYZ, Inc. When Tim explained to Max that his performance was unacceptable and that he, therefore, was ineligible to transfer, Max asked to be given a probationary period in which he assured Tim he would improve his performance enough to be considered for a transfer. *more details*

Max is not motivated to improve his performance in order to maintain his current work assignment but rather is hoping to improve his performance only to leave the department.

We have found in past circumstances that when Max has been counseled about his poor performance, improvement occurs. However, this improvement is short-lived, and invariably he reverts to his poor performance.

We feel that we have given Max ample opportunity to become a reliable long-term contributor to the department. We have given him feedback regarding his poor performance, and there is mutual agreement that he does not fit his assigned role and never will. Whereas we agree that there may be other jobs in XYZ, Inc. in which he could perform well, the purchasing department can ill afford to spend additional marginally productive months grooming him for transfer. *message*

Considering the above circumstances, we recommend that Max be given notice that his employment with the purchasing department will terminate May 6, 198–. *action*

If any outplacement assistance can be made available from Employee Relations, we request that this be done.

Please give me your comments regarding this matter at your earliest convenience.

MADE Format

Subject: Performance Problems and Recommended Termination of Max Perkins

Max Perkins, employed with XYZ Inc. since November 2, 198–, and now assigned to Purchasing, has a recurring performance problem related to the lack of detail given to his procurement responsibilities and his unusually large backlog of rejected-tubulars claims—outstanding claims of $3.5 million. Although he has been counseled about the need for improvement on several occasions by his previous supervisor Fred Boston and by me, he has made no long-term improvement. *message*

Max states he doesn't like the detail involved in the job and
thinks that the job was misrepresented to him. Although he now
wants to transfer to the Planning area, I have explained that we do
not transfer employees until performance in the present job is
satisfactory. There is mutual agreement that he cannot become a
long-term contributor to the department, and we cannot afford to
spend marginally productive months grooming him for transfer.

message

Therefore, I recommend that Max be given notice that his
employment with Purchasing will be terminated May 6, 198–.

Would you give me your comments regarding this situation at
your earliest convenience? Also, if you agree with the termination, would you see that he receives any available outplacement
assistance from Employee Relations?

action

The following summarizes the performance background,
ratings, merit increases, performance discussions and documentation of this employee:

Production (November 2, 198– to July 10, 198–), reporting to
Fred Boston: *A summary follows here of performance, reviews,
raises....*

Purchasing—Materials Control (July 10, 198– to November
198–), reporting to Alton James: *A summary follows here of
performance as compared to that of others in the department,
reviews, lack of raises, attitudes....*

Purchasing—Procurement (November 198– to present), reporting to me: *A summary follows here of performance as compared to
that of others, reviews, raises, attitudes...*

details

A copy of all performance appraisals and a list of salary increases and dates are attached for further review.

optional evidence

As you have noted from these examples, clarity is the primary reason
for the MADE format. In the first versions, the reader doesn't know
how to process the details until he or she has the punchline.

But there's another reason for the MADE format: time.

I've chosen this rather long version about Max's performance
problem specifically to illustrate how this need-to-know, MADE
format can save many readers much time. As soon as the reader's need
to know is satisfied, he or she can stop reading. The decision maker, in
this case probably the Director of Purchasing, may stop reading as soon
as he is convinced that Max should be terminated. If he is not convinced
after the opening "big-picture" message, he may continue to read the
who, when, where, why details and drop out at any time. If he still has

doubts about the termination and possible legal actions because of how the situation has been handled in the past, he may read through every single attachment. How much or how little to read is the reader's choice.

If this document is then passed on to Employee Relations with a "buck" slip from the decision maker, who has agreed with the termination, the Employee Relations reader can stop reading after she knows what action she is being asked to take. She probably will not care to read the details or attachments—or at least not until she gets ready to hold the outplacement discussions with Max.

Perhaps the previous supervisors of Max will be sent courtesy copies of the memo. If so, they will probably want to read only the message and recommendation for termination paragraphs just to be informed of the situation; they already know the details.

The "layered" effect of the MADE format closely follows that of news articles. The further you read, the more detail you get. Additionally, writers always find that once they think about what they want to say and summarize the big-picture message up front, many of the details, background, and introductory statements become altogether unnecessary.

You'll note that in the traditional versions, you did not know specifically what the writer wanted (how you should process the details you were getting) until the very end of the document. Then, after you got to the point of the communication, you had to go back and reread to reshuffle the details and reconsider them to see if the situation merited the recommended action.

Now, to make a further point for the reasons behind the MADE format: Which of the document versions above took less time to read, the traditional version of each pair or the MADE version? Right.

So, these are the primary reasons for using the MADE format: to reduce reading and writing time and to aid clarity.

The secondary benefits of the "message-up-front" format are almost as persuasive:

1) Clients and customers don't have to wade through the nonessential to get to the major benefits you can offer them.
2) Readers don't feel manipulated or teased into reading a lengthy proposal while you withhold the message and the action you want from them.

How can this time-saving format be used companywide? Simply have your memo stationery printed with the MADE acronym in the margin. A vice president of a large insurance company has done this for all those in all the departments reporting to him.

In addition, reports of almost any kind lend themselves to this set up: the message (overview, conclusions) comes first; the action (recommendations) comes second; the details (test methods, analysis, plans to accomplish the action, etc.) follow. Finally, the attachments or enclosures give optional information.

With all internal correspondence and reports organized in the same way, readers can trust the writers to put the punchline up front. If they stop reading early, they can rest assured that they haven't missed anything important. As a bonus, they save time in organizing the documents they write.

LET YOUR SUBORDINATES KNOW THEY CAN BE DIRECT WITH YOU

In Chapter 1, I mentioned several psychological reasons that explain why subordinates write long reports, one of which is to bury bad news. Help your employees realize that you don't have to be pampered and manipulated into their corner or conclusion. Let them know at the beginning of any writing task that you appreciate directness and that you encourage the MADE format for all kinds of memos and reports sent to you.

Finally, when you give the exception writing assignment that does require more detail, tell them at the beginning. Don't keep them guessing from assignment to assignment what detail you expect.

FOUR PRINCIPLES FOR CONCISENESS

In addition to this short-document format guide, here are four other principles for paring down documents and saving reading time:

Use Active-voice Verbs

In active-voice sentences, the subject of the sentence does the action of the verb. In passive-voice sentences, the subject receives the action.

Active: Joe approved the report. (four words)
Passive: The report was approved by Joe. (six words)
Active: Mary Climber scheduled the meeting for Friday. (seven words)
Passive: The meeting was scheduled for Friday by Mary Climber. (ten words)
Active: Please make the changes today. (five words)
Passive: It is requested that the changes be made today. (nine words)

Avoid Adjective and Adverb Clutter

Nouns and verbs are the words of fact—the words most important in business writing. Adjectives and adverbs are words of opinion; they both weaken and lengthen what you have to say.

Why write—

The inspiring speaker outlined a truly meaningful approach to the proper choice of candidates for that awesome responsibility. (18 opinionated words)

When you could say—

The speaker outlined a meaningful approach to choosing candidates for that responsibility. (12 factual-sounding words)

Dig Buried Verbs Out of Noun Phrases

Not:

This will provide for the *elimination* of the time for the *review* and *comparison* of bids. (16 words)

But:

This will *eliminate* time for *reviewing* and *comparing* bids. (eight words)

Avoid Circumlocutions, Clichés and Redundancies

Not:	But:
at this point in time	now
in view of the fact that	because
in my own personal opinion	in my opinion; I think
we will conduct an investigation into	we will investigate
it will be appreciated if	we will appreciate
it is suggested that	I suggest

The more time you spend condensing your documents, the less time it takes the 15 people on your distribution list to read them, the less secretarial time to type them, the less clerical time to reproduce and file them, and, finally, the less space to store them. Every paragraph and every page costs both time and money.

"I think we've got a form for that."

8
FORMS
USE
AND DESIGN

RECOMMENDATION: KNOW WHAT FORMS YOU HAVE;
KNOW WHY YOU HAVE THEM. USE THE NECESSARY;
DISCARD THE REST.

Most organizations are astounded to find out how many forms they have floating around the company. Records management experts say that it is not at all unusual to find twice as many forms as "those in the know" know the company has—sometimes up to 1,500-2,000 forms. They also estimate that it is not at all rare to find that at least 20 percent of the forms used in a company are completely unnecessary.

On first glance, forms seem to be the answer to everything. People feel they are helping gather the necessary information in a usable format on a timely basis, causing users as little pain as possible in that they don't have to compose an entire letter, memo or report to give the facts.

So why not forms and more forms?

WHAT DO FORMS COST?

Colonel Leonard Lee, internationally recognized records management expert and systems analyst, writes in *Records*

Management Quarterly (April 1982):

> The government has 3,947 approved generic categories of forms that list 676.2 million annual responses and consume 200 million hours in preparation time—and some 2,000 new forms are proposed by agencies for clearance each year to the government's approving authority (Office of Management and Budget). Small businesses alone file more than 305 million forms annually, comprising 850 million pages responding to 7.3 billion questions, and costing each of the firms an average of $1,270 to comply with requirements—a total of some $13 billion.... It is estimated that the bottom-line costs for doing governmental paperwork result in 2% to 5% of profits being drained from corporate revenues.

Forms designer John Burgess estimates the cost of processing forms to be at least 25 times the cost of the forms themselves. Studies show that for every business dollar spent on designing and printing a form, companies spend $20-$80 in processing and file maintenance.

Alfred J. Moran, president of the TJM Corporation, writes in *Financial Executive* (September 1982):

> The total U.S. market for business forms in 1980 was $4.3 billion. Theoretically applied to the U.S. market, a 10-percent cost reduction would result in approximately $430 million of potential actual savings on forms alone in one year. If one applies a 40:1 industry-adopted ratio of clerical costs to business forms expenditures, we are describing $17.2 billion annually in potential savings through increased efficiency in purchasing, storing, filling out, filing, retaining and destroying of business forms.

So when you start to design a form for some particular piece of information, don't simply consider the cost of printing the form. Instead, multiply that cost by 40 for a more accurate picture of how much the use of that form will cost you.

Are you sure you're not creating a form to collect information already available elsewhere?

WHERE DO ALL THE FORMS COME FROM AND WHERE DO THEY GO?

Chances are that if you catch a form in transit from one department to the next and try to trace it backward or follow it forward, those handling it will know only two steps in the life of the form—where it came from and where it goes. No more.

One manager in a public utility company began to ask "where and why" questions about the forms shuffled through his office. When he got few answers, he had an assistant do a flowchart for a five-copy form that particularly seemed to be going in circles. With much effort, he was able to cut the superfluous shuffling from an 18-step procedure to a four-step procedure as illustrated here:

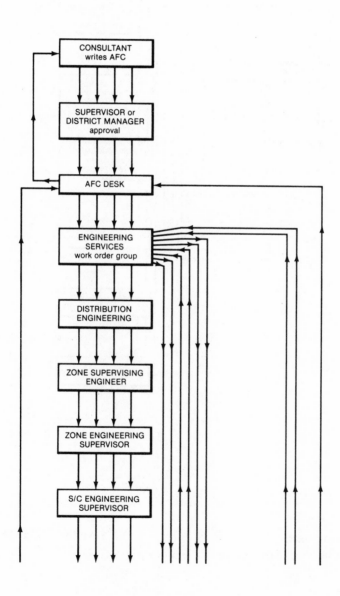

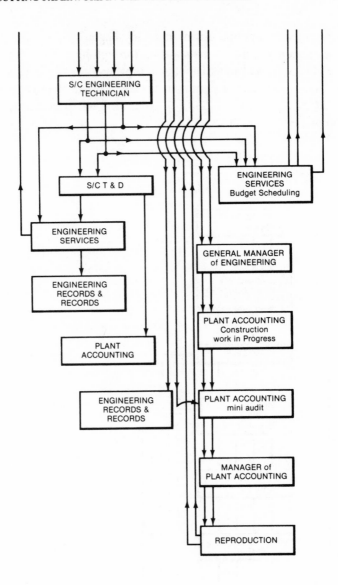

Figure 1:
A public utility company's forms audit revealed this 18-step procedure for five-copy work orders.

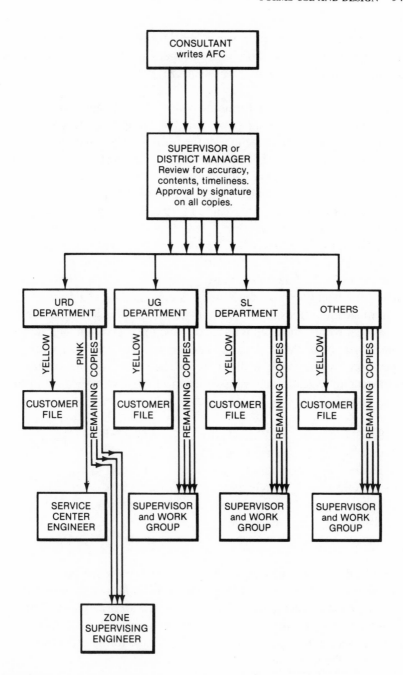

Figure 2:
The processing of the utility company's work orders was reduced to four steps.

If you ever intend to get the superfluous forms off your desk, then you need to do a forms audit. Forms-audit experts outline numerous ways to do such an overhaul of your business. Here are two of the most common methods:

The Numerical File. All forms are collected and arranged by number. Included in each file are samples of the form, correspondence about its creation, revised editions, who uses the form for what, and approximate number of forms used. The hair-pulling part of trying to set up a numerical file for audit is the confusion caused by wide gaps in the numbering system, forms with no numbers and forms with duplicate numbers.

The Functional Index. This kind of forms audit contains a sample of every form in the company that accomplishes the same purpose or that is related to the same operation. Frank Knox, in *Managing Paperwork: A Key to Productivity,* and Lee Grossman, in *Fat Paper,* point out the advantages of the functional index: It identifies forms as they relate to their corresponding procedures and systems, and it helps locate forms with misleading titles or without numbers or with unknown numbers.

In other words, the audit is based on function, operation, and subject. The subject is the thing, person, or procedure the form deals with. The operation is what you do with the form. The function is the purpose the form accomplishes. If you were to design a flowchart of the form, you'd have three headings:

SUBJECT	OPERATION	FUNCTION
equipment	specifications	to order
managers	training, status of	to report
stock clerks	attendance	to report
equipment	inspection	to instruct
stock plan	payment	to record
insurance	claims	to report

Still other forms auditors have other systems and methods, such as the personal interview, and chart the same information under these headings: Department, Activity, Document, Purpose. Trevor Bentley, in *Information, Communication, and the Paperwork Explosion,* calls this interviewer the "pathfinder." The aim of the forms-use interview is to answer the questions: What? Who? Where? When? Why? How?

However you chose to do the audit to locate whatever paperwork you have flowing around, the audit activity guides you to do a major overhaul of your paperwork system. This information, however collected, should enable you to trace and analyze the paperflow, to pinpoint problems (such as duplication of effort, superfluous information, unnecessary documents, delayed paperflow), and then to develop alternatives. The alternative may be a new path for the information; a better-designed form; a combining of forms that needlessly collect the same collect the same information; the elimination of unnecessary information, processing, or recording.

In addition to helping you reduce paperwork and cut costs, such forms audits can be instructive: Your employees, especially new ones, don't have to guess at why they do what they do. To see the whole picture on a flowchart helps them locate their own cog in the company wheel and thus gain an appreciation for accuracy and thoroughness in their work.

WHERE AND WHEN TO USE FORMS

After seeing the spiraling cost of forms and their management, do you dare create new ones?

Yes. Forms can help you reduce the time spent in composing routine correspondence and in supplying or requesting routine information.

For example, consider creating the following form documents:

- brochures (for giving customers and particularly your own employees information about your products and services). If the brochure is properly designed, you don't need a cover letter to say what you're sending.
- newsletters/circulars (for eliminating numerous phone calls from isolated employees who need to be updated frequently on certain aspects of the business). Tell users to destroy them after use rather than have them clutter the files for posterity.
- instructions for operating equipment (to eliminate repeating the same directions innumerable times). Post the instructions by the equipment used.
- training/instructions (to eliminate the need to repeat the same orientation to each new employee). Put instructions in three-ring binders so they can be easily updated, and keep only a few copies to eliminate the need of updating numerous copies.
- internal correspondence (to collect routine data and to send reminders and follow-ups). Use preprinted memos with check-off boxes for what you are sending, requesting or questioning.

When you find out that these form documents aren't accomplishing their purpose, redesign them or eliminate them altogether.

Now that sounds obvious, doesn't it? But I hear people make comments like the following about their form reminders or information-gathering memos: "Nobody ever gets this information right. I don't know why we use this form letter. You see this question? They always give us the gross instead of the net. It doesn't say that here and it's confusing. Half of these people we have to call up anyway to get what we really need."

Yet, it never seems to dawn on these people to rewrite or redesign their confusing, inefficient forms!

GUIDELINES FOR GOOD FORM DESIGN

Lest you think designing a form can be done in 10 minutes, think again. Before you begin, consider the following:

- company specifications about size of form
- artwork necessary for layout
- printing arrangements and costs
- storage and inventory control of the blank forms
- distribution to respondents, including addressing and mailing
- collection of responses
- data processing and entry into computer or onto a paper record
- summarizing and reassembling the information in some usable form

The following are tips collected from numerous experts in the forms-design field:

- Give the form a title that clearly signals its purpose.
- Give the form a number for better control.
- Consider the weight and grade of the paper to make sure it is suitable for the intended handling. Will all carbon copies be readable? Will photocopies be readable?
- Include instructions with the form.
- Tell where the form came from and where the respondent is supposed to send it.
- Put the key data items in the easiest-to-read positions.
- Place the items in the same order as they will need to be entered on other forms or into the computer.

- Break information into logical sections.
- Use color or shading to separate sections.
- Use color coding for copies to be routed to different places.
- Leave adequate space to enter the requested information—whether entered by typewriter or manually.
- Leave adequate space for all signatures.
- Use complete terms. (Don't say "quarter." Do you mean "reporting quarter" or "sales quarter"? Don't say "time." Do you mean "time of accident" or "time of notification to company"?)
- Use the same terms for the same items on the form. (Don't call something a "warehouse" and then later on the form refer to the same thing as "storage site.")
- Try to avoid open-ended questions. Instead, print answer choices with check boxes. Put the boxes to be checked before the items rather than after.
- Use simple words and short sentences with the item titles and explanations. (Don't say "Where did you obtain the equipment?" when you can say "Where did you get the projector?" Don't say "This percentage rate will accrue to your account," when you can say "This interest will be added to your account.")
- Give instructions about where and how to include additional, unusual explanations about various items.
- Give a department or position title to contact for questions about the form.

Remember that most forms should be designed by experienced layout people. Don't decide to design by chance.

As a rule-of-thumb about creating new forms: Watch out for duplication of effort. Forms may already exist to gather the same information to be used in slightly different ways. Be aware of the hidden costs in forms; it's not the single cost of paper and printing that hurts, but approximately *40* times that cost for distribution, processing, storage, and retrieval of the information gathered.

FORMS FOR INTERNAL CORRESPONDENCE

If you're designing form correspondence for internal use (keep external form correspondence to an absolute minimum), use the MADE format described in Chapter 7 and ask: What's the bottom-line message or purpose? What action do you want or plan to take based on the message? What details need elaboration—who, when, where, why, how, how much? What optional evidence is enclosed or attached to make the message easier to understand or the action easier to take? That's it. End the document.

Spend the time you save on the internal form memo to write a personal, goodwill-building or sales letter to a customer or client.

FORMS FOR EXTERNAL CORRESPONDENCE

If you must use form correspondence outside your organization, don't make it sound like a form. Of course, when you deal with the same inquiries or problems, you will develop basic letter content; but with the use of a computer, you can tailor those basic ideas for each customer. (Inserting a customer name in the text in three or four places is *not* customizing.) Your customers should not be aware that the letters they receive are form documents. Just a few variations in wording make the customer-reader feel as though the letter is addressed to his or her questions or needs.

Make your customers feel valued and appreciated as individuals rather than as account numbers. Lavish the time saved from internal paperwork on goodwill chats with or letters to the people who pay for your products or your services.

"You may as well send them a copy; it can't hurt."

9
DISTRIBUTION
LISTS

RECOMMENDATION: GET OFF OTHERS' DISTRIBUTION
LISTS AND TAKE THEM OFF YOURS.

For the last 15 years, career couselors and management consultants telling people how to climb the corporate ladder have emphasized that information is power. Their advice? Get on as many distribution lists as possible; the more you know, the better chance you have to usurp someone else's authority or have a say in the decision-making process. At best, they explain, you will have a say in everything going on in the company; at the least, everyone will learn your name.

People have taken such advice to heart, and now corporate desks everywhere are snowed with paper about everything from the company's baseball league standing to an impending merger.

WHY GET OFF DISTRIBUTION LISTS?

True, information can be power, but *paper* is not necessarily information. (See Chapter 13 for tips on how to manage information in forms other than paper.)

So what's the harm of a copy here and a copy there?

Costs Are Staggering

Business forms experts Alfred J. Moran (*Financial Executive*, September 1982) and W. James Russell (*The Office*, May 1984) cite studies by the National Business Forms Association to say that 70 percent of the white-collar worker's time is spent processing paperwork. That includes preparing, recording, interpreting, filing, and maintaining information.

In addition to the reading, processing, and filing time your documents cost others, consider the cost of storing what you send: about $2,160 annually for each active four-drawer file cabinet of 18,000 pages. Of all the documents retained, 85 percent are never referred to again. And 45 percent of file documents are duplicate copies. Therefore, we could cut annual records maintenance cost by 45 percent simply by staying away from the copy machine.

When people show up at the photocopier, they tend to think: "He said to make 20 copies; I guess 25 should do it—that'll be better than having to walk back to the machine if we're short." This reasoning doesn't take into consideration all the other costs (besides walking to the copier) involved in those five extra copies. When those five copies aren't used, they have to go somewhere—into the files or into the trashbasket, both a waste of money. But even when you do use those five copies by adding five names to your distribution list, you're not simply paying for five sheets of paper. You're paying for the time for those papers to be read, processed, filed, and maintained.

Too Much Is Confusing

An administrative assistant in the education center of an international computer company says her boss insists that she send all announcements of new course offerings to all branch offices for distribution. The problem? Only a select few each year are eligible for a particular course. But rather than pare down the distribution list to those branches that are eligible, the boss instead insists that she continue to send all branches a copy of the announcement.

The result? Every time the announcement goes out, the administrative assistant is flooded with calls from those people confused about who can attend. Their question: If we're ineligible to attend, why did we get a copy of the announcement? Every time the course is announced, her distribution list costs her about eight hours on the phone; in addition, each caller wastes time on the inquiry.

Most Are Ignored

In addition to cost, however, copies sent to everybody who has any need to know before the year 2000 turn people off. Frequently I hear thumbnail sketches about employees who copy everybody on everything: "He's the kind of guy who cc's everybody in the company on everything he does."

We've all read the books on corporate politics and learned how to "flag our accomplishments." Now people are on to the tactic and want the flags lowered to half-mast.

Some argue that they send copies as a courtesy to keep others informed. Is it really courtesy or is it laziness in paring down the list to who really needs to know? Yes, I know some people will get paranoid as their name disappears from distribution lists, but if the campaign to cut paperwork grows companywide, reason will eventually win out.

The Trivial Buries the Important

My survey reveals that the average white-collar worker receives 145 pages per week. The survey also verifies that much goes unread. People simply can't keep up with the reading load. Surveys done by Dr. Phyllis A. Miller, consultant with Reading Development Seminars, also show that the higher one progresses in the company, the heavier the reading load. The result, of course, is that most paperwork gets skimmed and little gets read.

The more you send to any particular person, the less attention any of it gets. More important, the reader begins to doubt your basic understanding of what's important and what's too trivial to bother others about.

If you don't believe that few people read the mass distributions you send, try a follow-up call with a question or two. I'll bet your conversation will go something like this:

Writer: I was just wondering if you got my memo on the Casper project.

Reader: Uh, yeah, I think I saw it. (Shuffles through desk to locate it.)

Writer: I was just calling to see if you thought you could have figures to me by Friday.

Reader: By Friday? Oh, I didn't know you were going to need them that soon.

Writer: Yeah, as I said in the memo [hurumps], I need them for the operational study due next Tuesday.

Reader: Somehow I missed that. Listen, how about Monday? Could I...?

The effect of the mass memo-distribution list is much like that of the "Dear Occupant" junk mail most of us get. Despite the introduction of the word processor and the LOCATE and REPLACE key that inserts "Mr. Smith" every fourth line in the text, readers still recognize and largely ignore junk mail. Mass distribution lists in the office get little more respect or attention than they do at home.

Copies Demand a Response

Not only do those with long distribution lists waste others' reading time, but also these distributors often expect their readers to respond. Their memos usually begin, "Please review and give your comments about the enclosed...." Thus the distributed paper begets more paper. Additionally, the waiting time for all the responses to come in—or the wait to see that the responses are not coming in—delays the writer's further action or necessitates a follow-up call such as that mentioned earlier.

Copies Air Your Dirty Linen

Distribution lists are the tools of paper wars. Recently, I witnessed such a war between colleagues over a new product brochure. Data from branch directors, marketing, the project manager and the editor/writer had been shuffled for so long that the final brochure was long overdue, but no one was clearly to blame. However, the project manager began to get heat from his boss about the deadline, so he, in turn, began to put things in writing. That is, he expressed his exasperation about the deadline and threatened to reassign the project altogether, with copies to all those who sided with him because they knew of the difficulty in gathering data from all those branch offices with input to the project.

That, of course, prompted a memo from the boss (the opposition) lamenting the sensitivity of the project manager in being upset by the prospect of reassignment. The opposition sent copies, of course, to all the individuals on the distribution list of the project manager, along with a few new names of those siding with the boss about the failure of the project manager to meet the deadline.

To put it simply: They both sounded like tattling sixth graders.

But amusement in the eye of the receiver is not the only danger. Paper wars often create much more dire consequences: completely sabotaged projects.

In summary: Distribution lists cost money, upstage more important ideas, demand responses, get ignored, cause confusion, and make the paper warriors look silly.

What to do about eliminating or at least restricting distribution?

ESTABLISH GUIDELINES FOR WHO SHOULD GET COPIES

Make it a big deal to send a copy of anything. Choose recipients carefully. Make sure they really want a copy, need a copy, know what to do with the copy, don't already have the same information available elsewhere, and don't have access to anyone else's copy of your document.

To be repetitious: Remember that it's not the cost of paper but the cost of preparing, reading, processing, filing, and maintaining the paper.

Ask Recipients If They Really Need Copies

A report going to a certain department often outlives its usefulness to that department. But the receiver often never thinks to notify the sender; rather, he or she simply tosses the report aside or, worse yet, into the files—untouched.

Every six months or year, ask those who continue to receive a copy of what you send to verify their need. Attach a note and ask for their signature and return of the note if they still have a use for it. If you don't hear from them, chances are they didn't even read your note.

Remove from Your List Those Who Don't Respond to Inquiries about the Need to Know

You may try a stronger tactic. If those on your distribution list don't respond to your note asking if they still need your document, simply remove them from the list until you hear otherwise. If people don't complain, they haven't been reading the report and they won't even know it's no longer arriving in their in-basket.

Help People Route What You Write

Send along a list of names with your document and ask the first reader to initial and pass the information on to the next person on the list. School teachers, who are already snowed under with papers to grade, often use this method. One memo attached to a clip board is handed from teacher to teacher as they initial it and send the information on down the corridor.

Put a Log Sheet by Your Copier

Force people to record their sins of distribution by using a charge-back system for each department. Keep a clipboard with columns for name, department, use, and number of copies to be expensed. At least this record will cut down on personal use of the machine. And many businesses have found that this record makes people stop and think before they punch out 25 collated copies when they really need 15.

Post Information of General Interest

Practically every office building has bulletin boards near restrooms, water fountains, or lounge areas. Most, however, contain the same announcements that have been posted for months.

Instead of long distribution lists, use these boards to communicate information that needs to be communicated to many people: job announcements, welcomes to new employees, companywide or departmentwide meetings, educational opportunities, new project announcements, sales figures—whatever it is that you use mass mailings for in your organization.

Let your employees know that you really intend to use these boards for communication rather than decoration. They'll learn to check them as regularly as they go to the restroom or lounge.

"Uh, ... ah, ... I guess my secretary didn't catch that. I'll have to talk to her."

10
HOW TO GET
THE MOST FROM YOUR
SECRETARIAL
SUPPORT STAFF

RECOMMENDATION: PERMIT YOUR SECRETARY TO
HANDLE THE ROUTINE PAPERWORK. IF SHE ISN'T
CAPABLE, TRAIN HER, REPLACE HER, OR COMPOSE YOUR
OWN DOCUMENTS ON A COMPUTER.

(Note: Because over 99 percent of all secretaries in this country are female, I will use the feminine pronoun when referring to secretaries or clerk-typists. However, the comments in this chapter apply equally to males holding clerical, secretarial, or administrative assistant positions.)

HOW MUCH TIME DO YOU AND YOUR
SECRETARY SPEND ON PAPERWORK?

In my survey of 657 white-collar workers, they estimated that they spend an average of 44 percent of their time on the job reading and writing. A breakdown by job classification follows:

	Reading	Writing	Total
Senior managers	24%	22%	46%
Middle managers	23%	22%	45%

Professionals with no supervisory responsibilities	18%	22%	40%
Administrative assistants	30%	24%	54%
Secretaries/clerks	32%	18%	50%

In the earlier-cited 1982 Booz, Allen, & Hamilton survey of 300 knowledge workers who actually kept contemporaneous records, researchers found that these workers spent 21 percent of their time reading and writing. Although those who completed my own surveys were not scientifically selected and percentage answers may have been overestimated by the participants, the discrepancy in the findings of the two surveys does point to a major underlying perception (and reality)—the perception of employees that they are bogged down in paperwork.

Whichever survey figures you use, paperwork costs from 21 percent to 44 percent of your white-collar payroll. In organizations that are more paper-heavy than most, such as insurance companies and banks, the percentage rises drastically. The clerical workforce is growing two-and-one-half times faster than the rest of the workforce. It has moved from the fourth largest to the largest segment of the white-collar workforce—about 19 million workers. And the Bureau of Labor Statistics estimated that employment in this category would increase 29 percent from 1982 to 1995.

To make the cost of paperwork specific to you and your secretary, ask her to keep a record of how much time she spends dealing with paperwork. In other words, she should *not* record time spent on the telephone, with visitors, with co-workers, with taking instructions from you. Rather, have her record how much time it takes her to handle the following: incoming and outgoing mail, typing, filing, retrieving files, taking dictation, making copies, filling out forms, collecting data for reports. Be sure to tell her you are not necessarily checking up on her speed but that you simply want to get an accurate picture of the time spent on paperwork in your department.

After your secretary has kept track of how many hours she spends weekly on paperwork and you have multiplied that time by her weekly wage, estimate how many hours each week *you* spend on paperwork. Multiply that percentage by your salary.

How much can you save by shifting half of your paperwork load to your secretary?

IS THE SECRETARY CAPABLE?

Obviously, it costs less for your secretary to fill out a form or write a letter than for you to do it. But the bigger question in the minds of most bosses is: Do I want to risk my reputation on her skills?

Of the 657 employees surveyed, 485 said they have someone else who types for them. When asked to classify the editing skills of those secretaries and typists, they responded this way:

- 18% rated those skills "excellent"
- 44% rated those skills "good"
- 27% rated those skills "fair"
- 10% rated those skills "poor"

Over one-third of the supervisors cannot confidently depend on their secretaries to handle their paperwork adequately. That means either that bosses have to clean up the paperwork after their secretaries or that they have to handle the important administrative paperwork themselves!

Secretaries are aware of their own deficiencies in the area of writing and paperwork. In my secretarial writing workshops, the participants frequently list their knowledge of grammar as their weakest area. And yet that's where their primary responsibilities lie—in typing, proofreading, and editing their superior's correspondence and reports for grammar and clarity.

The Secretary (April 1984) reports the following results of a year-long study, involving 50 companies and 16 states, recently completed by MPC Educational Publishers. Companies were asked to list in order of priority basic skills for entry-level secretarial jobs. Language and communication skills were second on the list, right after typing/ keyboarding skills. Yet, only 12 percent of the companies tested for language skills before hiring. And only 8 percent tested for editing skills! In other words, just because you have a secretary, don't assume that she can handle her primary responsibilities. Chances are that nobody has asked her or tested her on these skills and that she hasn't made any claims concerning them.

Yet in the same study, almost every company commented on the need to upgrade their secretaries' basic language skills, including grammar, spelling, and punctuation, and their oral and written communication skills.

Other consulting groups, schools, governmental agencies and testing centers confirm the decline in basic skills among all graduates across the nation. SAT scores have dropped over the past 20 years. We now have an estimated 23 million illiterate adults in the United States.

Obviously, your organization has not intentionally hired any of these illiterate adults as secretaries. But the above facts do tell you that because fewer and fewer high school and college graduates have good basic skills you can no longer take for granted that a secretary has strong, or even adequate, proofreading or editing skills.

To give you an idea of these deficiencies in secretarial skills, I've listed below some of the questions asked of me by secretaries during workshops:

- Is "review" a preposition?
- If you don't know where to use commas, wouldn't it be safer just to leave them all out?
- Why isn't "Because of my varied experience" a sentence?
- Do you put commas after the street and the zip code in the inside address of a letter?
- What's a pronoun?
- When do you capitalize "i" when you're referring to yourself?

If you have made the assumption that all secretaries have adequate editing or proofreading skills, you're taking a terrible risk with your reputation both inside and outside the company.

A secretary can sabotage your time, money, and image in several ways: 1) inaccurate work: wrong or missing details; statistical, grammatical, and clarity errors; 2) sloppy work: work that looks as if she had lunch over it or sent out a rough draft by mistake; 3) wasted time or materials.

If your secretary turns out inaccurate work, pinpoint the cause. Are you giving inadequate directions? Are you withholding other resources—books, information, or resource people—for her to use to check her work? If either is the case, the solution is simple. Give her a chance to tell you what further direction she needs from you and what information and resources are missing.

If grammatical and proofreading skills are weak, the solution is more difficult. Grammar and proofreading courses can help secretaries make tremendous improvements by refreshing them on basic sentence structure and common grammatical errors. Awareness and self-study reviews can bring "fair" and "good" editing skills up to where they should be—"excellent."

But if your secretary has extremely poor editing skills, you will need to see that she gets extensive help in night school at a local university or through private tutoring. In the typical 16-hour grammar or writing course offered on site at your business, she cannot hope to master the necessary skills to assume your total communication and paperwork load. Grammatical structure is too technical to be learned from scratch in just a few hours.

Second, if the secretary's work is unacceptable because it is sloppy, perhaps you haven't impressed upon her what is at stake: her reputation and tenure in the company—as well as yours. If words don't help, then sloppiness is a trait you don't have time to help her extinguish on the job.

Finally, if the problem falls in the last category—wasted time and materials—you can correct the situation several ways. The first thing is to tell her what has to be perfect and what doesn't. If you have a conscientious secretary who always does things right, she may be typing forms that could be done more quickly and easily by hand, typing responses that could be handled by a buck slip, and retyping reports to the file simply because the margin is a quarter-inch too narrow.

Because perfection is difficult to find, you don't want to discourage it in general but simply on occasion, for productivity reasons. Not all tasks demand perfection. Be sure to let her know which do and which don't so that she can spend her time on the most important.

Time-management and personal-effectiveness courses can adequately teach secretaries how to arrange their schedules to make both your time and their time more productive. In fact, for further information, see *The New Secretary: How to Handle People As Well As You Handle Paper*, Chapter 20 (Facts On File, 1985).

Additionally, since a boss can either work with or against his or her secretary, learn to use your secretary more effectively with some of the following suggestions.

WHAT A SECRETARY SHOULD BE ABLE TO DO FOR YOU AND HOW TO HELP HER DO IT

Perhaps you've never had a highly skilled secretary and don't know that this assistant should be able to:

Proofread and Edit. A secretary should be able to proofread and edit all correspondence and reports for grammatical errors, clarity problems, and accuracy in names and numbers. Often secretaries tell me that they notice grammatical or clarity problems in a poorly constructed sentence but that their boss does not give them opportunity to change—or even question—these matters. Granted, a secretary unfamiliar with technical content can rewrite a sentence or paragraph to correct it and completely change the intended meaning. Therefore, you should not give a secretary carte blanche to change what you've written without having her call your attention to the changes.

But you should give her permission to question. Ask her to pencil a question mark in the margin beside sentences that seem unclear to her and beside sentences she has reworded to eliminate a grammatical error.

Set Up Report Formats. A secretary should be able to take raw information from the computer or from your rough draft of a speech or report and set it up in an easy-to-read format with proper paragraphing, lists, and headings. You can help her do this by providing copies of old forms or reports as models. But also be aware that old documents may not necessarily be prepared in the most readable, usable format. Allow her leeway to turn a long paragraph into a bulleted list or to add headings with informative captions where these will improve readability and clarity.

Complete Forms. A secretary should be able to fill out forms and routine reports. Again, you should give her some idea of where to find a sample and where to find a resource person to answer her questions. Then point out any differences between this new form or report and the previous ones given as models—*before* she completes the task.

Compose Routine Correspondence from Models. A secretary should be able to compose your routine correspondence. As you read incoming memos and letters, you should write in the margin your answers to any questions or requests for information. Then, following the MADE outline presented in Chapter 7 of this book, the secretary should be able to compose a draft of the correspondence for you to sign. If the correspondence requires more than a few answers to simple questions, simply refer her to a similar response as a model and then tell her what the exceptions are for this specific writing task.

For example, let's say a request for a proposal on a specific piece of equipment comes to your office—a proposal to which you don't want to respond. Your secretary should be able to put together a draft of a letter for you to work with (or perhaps even to sign, ready to go out) and all you should have to say to her is something like:

> Sheryl, here's an RFP that there's no point in our bidding on. Follow that last "no" letter we sent to Heinken Corporation, but

substitute this reason: Tell them we have such a backlog on orders that we could not possibly install equipment within the 15 days they've specified.

Other bosses keep a manual of basic correspondence. The secretary can simply flip through the manual and choose a letter or memo to use as a model, making substitutions where necessary. If you don't have such a manual or similar form documents on your computer already, begin developing them. Every time you write something patently "typical," instruct your secretary to note it for later reference as a model.

Many top-notch secretaries learn their boss's style and business so well that they prepare and attach responses to incoming mail, ready for the boss's signature.

Collect Data for Your Writing. On complex paperwork tasks, a secretary should be able to anticipate your needs and to collect necessary data for you from the computer, from the files, and from other resource people. She can present the collected information to you at once, and you can have it at your fingertips as you draft or dictate your own document.

Help your secretary be productive by telling her what is important and what doesn't demand perfection. As a college student on my first secretarial job (before the days of word processors), I spent hours retyping routine real estate forms to eliminate all signs of liquid paper changes or flying caps. Today, I receive contracts with smudges, initialed changes, and all kinds of write-in comments. Back then, because my reputation as a secretary was at stake, I spent valuable time and attention on the typing of routine documents. Make sure your secretary knows which documents must be perfect and which aren't worth the trouble.

Finally, set up a list of priorities for your specific attention. Tell your secretary what paperwork you prefer to handle yourself and what you want her to handle. Depending on her experience and on how you rate her competence, you may want to review her documents before she sends them out, or have her report to you only after the fact. Permitting a secretary to sign her own name gives her a feeling of ownership and pride in the work (as discussed in Chapter 3) and often encourages her to improve her composition skills.

Proofreading and editing? Setting up formats? Filling out forms and routine reports? Composing correspondence? Collecting data? All this from a secretary? Yes.

And when you find a secretary who is capable of these tasks, pay her what she's worth. According to the Administrative Management

Society, the weekly salary in effect as of January 1985, for a level B secretary was $283; for a level A secretary, $316; for an executive secretary/administrative assistant, $368. If your salary schedule doesn't match or exceed these, why not? After all, a secretary can increase your own productivity considerably.

In fact, keep up with the hours you now spend on paperwork without depending on your secretary for the above skills. Then train her, assign her these tasks (don't forget the learning curve), and see how many more free hours you have to sell, think, make decisions, or whatever it is you do.

GETTING ALONG WITHOUT A SECRETARY

For some people, having a secretary is a status symbol. If that's the reason you have one, then skip this section. If you have a secretary only to deal with co-workers or visitors, and if she fulfills that role adequately, then give her the budget and authority to hire a clerk to handle the paperwork.

But if you've hired a secretary to help you with the paperwork and she isn't capable of doing that, then train her, replace her, or do without her. A secretary with poor or fair editing and writing skills *isn't* better than none at all. She can ruin your reputation—and perhaps your sale—by casting doubt on the accuracy of everything coming from your office or your company.

So what do you do without a secretary?

Learn to use a computer yourself. I know that books written a few years back, and directed to women who expected to be taken seriously in the business world, advised upwardly mobile professionals never to learn to type, or at least never to let their skill be known. Supposedly, typing branded them as nonexecutive material. Nonsense.

It's not only the headhunters and career consultants who have pushed this peculiar idea. After the "real" books on the bestseller list of some time ago (*Real Men Don't Eat Quiche; Real Women Don't Pump Gas,* etc.), some may wonder if "real" professionals compose their own documents. Yes. I work with top professionals in numerous industries and positions who are computer literate and who compose their complex documents themselves—and get a more creative, more organized, more complete document in fewer drafts than would be necessary with secretarial typing assistance.

The manager of a large accounting firm, who caught one of his top accountants composing his audit report on the computer, had this to say: "We don't pay professionals around here to use a word processor. Have a secretary do that." The chagrined accountant, who passed on this boss's comment to me, insisted that he could turn out a better report much more quickly if he wrote it himself on the word processor.

Other professionals agree. According to my survey (excluding those professionals who were employed by a computer company and had more access and motivation to use a computer in their writing), 25 percent of the white-collar professionals and managers say they compose their own documents on computer. Adia Personnel Services in Menlo Park, California, also recently completed a study, reported in *Training and Development Journal* (July 1985), revealing that of nearly 1,000 companies in eight countries, 24 percent of the executives have computers on their desks. (This latter study, however, did not ask employees directly if they used their computers to compose their own documents, as mine did.) But these two studies do show a fairly steady increase over the 5 to 10 percent figures given just a few years ago.

Companies that have computers on the desks of most of their white-collar employees are finding that professionals can think better, organize their thoughts more easily, and be more creative on the computer than they can with dictating equipment or with pen. A second important advantage is quick access to information without waiting for manual retrieval from the files. (More about that in Chapter 13.)

First of all, the average person speaks about 150-180 words a minute, types 40-50 words a minute, and writes in longhand about 20-30 words a minute. So composing on the computer is faster than in longhand. (These figures assume you know what you want to say in the document. And you should—if you've followed the planning steps given in Chapter 7.)

Second, because a word processor is faster, the writing style tends to be conversational rather than clichéd, formal and stuffy.

Third, computers can help you think. You can easily throw a random list of ideas on the screen, see what points you need to cover, and then reshuffle those ideas into logical order. In other words, you can see your plan before you work it. You can sketch out the rough draft and capture your main ideas by simply setting up headings of main points and subpoints. Then, after you see the whole framework of the document and determine the most logical arrangement, you can fill in the flesh around the skeleton.

One final advantage the computer has over longhand or dictation is that you can see what you have to say exactly as it will appear on the page. You can tell when paragraphs are getting too long, when a list will be more readable and effective than a paragraph, when a graph will emphasize and clarify key points.

If secretaries were the only, or even the best, way to go, why wouldn't bestselling authors, who deal almost exclusively in words, use secretaries to write their books? From media profiles on writers, I know of only a very few who dictate books to a secretary. Writers have found the typewriter or the word processor to be the most efficient method of writing.

But now the problem—not enough computers on the desks of those who can use them to best advantage. While the earlier-cited Adia study found that 24 percent of executives have computers on their desks, 84 percent of all U.S. secretaries do. Therefore, it is primarily the lower-level employees who are now taking advantage of office automation.

If you're a manager, become computer literate. If you hold the organizational purse strings, provide computers.

UPGRADING YOUR CLERICAL STAFF

Should organizations do away with clerical staff altogether? Of course not. Some organizations hire secretaries and administrative assistants to handle people on the phone and in person. If your secretaries are competent in these skills, fine.

But I say that because so much office work involves paper, organizations should make sure the clerical staff that handles this paper is competent, accurate, conscientious, and time-efficient. Otherwise, the company pays for most jobs to be done twice—by the secretary and by the supervisor/boss.

Before you hire your next secretary, make sure you test her in basic skills—and I don't mean just a typing test. Twenty years ago, a high school diploma meant basic reading, writing, and math skills. That's no longer true and no knowledgeable person will argue that with you.

The personnel department, or whoever is responsible for hiring, should test paperwork skills—grammar, spelling, use of resource books, simple math—and screen applicants accordingly. Secretaries who are already working but who lack these basic skills should be informed of these deficiencies in their performance reviews, given training on company time, and allowed a probationary period to improve these skills on their own. Certainly, companies should purchase the appropriate materials for self-study programs for those secretaries motivated to keep their current jobs and improve their skills for whatever future jobs they may hold.

And before you tell me what a shortage of secretaries we'd soon have if you applied these screening and training measures, let me say that no one is more aware of that probable shortage than I am.

But, perhaps, when the shortage becomes acute, competent workers will be attracted to the job of secretary and get paid what they are worth to the organization—not what their boss is worth. Most organizations still tie secretarial salaries to the rank of the professional they support. What kind of incentive is that for a secretary to improve her skills?

A one-time executive secretary at a public utility company reports disgustedly that she recently had a salary decrease and a title change back to senior secretary, all because her boss was demoted. If her salary isn't linked to her performance, why should she work on self-improvement? When a secretary adequately supports a "rising star" who recognizes her paperwork skills and takes her up the corporate ladder, that's fine. "Salary level by professional supported" encourages boss-secretary teamwork. But the reverse—demotion—should not be true.

Finally, higher salaries, of course, encourage competency. In the interim, while we work to improve secretaries' basic language competencies, companies should not suffer from staggering clerical overhead cost, the confusion caused by undetected errors in internal correspondence and reports, and perhaps irreparable harm to relationships and sales caused by an unqualified clerical staff handling paperflow to customers.

Find or train clerical staff competent to handle the routine, necessary paperwork.

11
WRITING
TRAINING

RECOMMENDATION: LEARN TO WRITE AND TEACH
YOUR SUBORDINATES TO WRITE.

Top-down training, in addition to permitting senior managers to improve their communication skills, sends a strong message to others throughout the company: "This company cares how you write. Our products, our services, and our credentials depend on communication in all forms."

PRACTICE DOESN'T MAKE PERFECT

Some people think that good writing, like breathing, is instinctive or, at least, that these skills develop naturally. Well, you may learn to talk by talking, but you don't learn to write by writing—especially by writing incorrectly. Practicing bad writing habits only ingrains weaknesses and makes it more difficult to shed incorrect techniques and phrases in favor of appropriate ones.

An unpublished writer sitting across the table from me at a writers conference confessed that she had 16 completed novels. "One of these days, I'm going to break into print. I just know it. I've gotten the nicest rejection letters from editors." I wasn't so brash as to tell her that she should have spent the equivalent time studying the techniques of her craft rather than repeat the mistakes of the first novel 15 times. Had she done so, I am convinced she would have been a lot further along toward her goal.

Likewise, you'd be surprised at how many managers think that because they do a lot of paperwork they have adequate writing skills. The truth of the situation may be that these managers continue to write more and to create more paperwork for themselves or their subordinates precisely because they do not fully understand the writing process.

Training specialists, perhaps more than any other group, recognize and laugh about the but-they-should-have-sent-my-boss lament almost always forthcoming in company training classes—almost always from participants who have been "nominated" to attend classes, rather than those who have signed up on their own. Frequently they're right. "They" *should have* sent the boss.

The *Training and Development Journal* (1980) reports a study done by Joe Thomas and Peter Sireno to identify competencies considered most important for managers in various industries. After a literature review and suggestions from employers and consultants, the researchers identified 115 activities to be included on their questionnaires sent to a random sample of firms in various industries. All responses were gathered into three functional areas: communication, leadership and control.

The most frequently cited, necessary competencies were in the area of communication. The most frequently cited communication skills were related to the exchange of information or instructions with supervisors, peers, and subordinates.

An example of such an exchange: At a breakfast to kick off a writing workshop set up for his staff, a manager gave me a copy of his course announcement memo so that I could learn the names of the attendees from his distribution list. The first line of his memo read:

> "A writing skills enhancement workshop has been scheduled for all personnel in the accounting department to help enhance writing skills."

For the remainder of the two days, every time I heard the comment, "But you don't know Fred (the boss/manager); he'd change this to read...," I believed it.

I have never met or read about a professional writer who thinks he or she has perfected writing skills to the point that there is no room for improvement. Instead, I hear comments such as, "The book was the best job I could do at that point in my development." Or, "Thank God for good editors." Yet, I do hear training specialists lament the fact that often the bosses in their organizations see no need for updating their own skills—only the skills of their subordinates.

That is not to say, of course, that senior-level managers never avail themselves of writing training. They do. And writing training in their organizations is most effective. When the top executives are already good writers, they usually don't have to be persuaded to improve their skills; they know the value of good writing. They're much like tennis pros who are always on the court practicing their serve.

But there are advantages to across-the-board writing training other than improved customer communication. When everyone learns to write in appropriate business formats and style, the write/edit/rewrite/ edit/rewrite paper-shuffling syndrome is minimized. Second, when both boss and subordinate are trained to write in the same formats with attention to the right questions and answers, bosses can trust subordinates to handle more of the paperwork. Finally, with similar formats and good writing for internal documents, everybody saves reading time.

REASONS FOR POOR WRITING

The primary reason, I have already stated: Our educational system has failed in teaching the basics. But that's beside the point for the individual manager on the job who has responsibility for teaching herself and the remainder of the staff to write.

So let's begin there—with reasons managers can actually do someing about.

Reason 1: Lazy thinking. To write clearly, people have to think clearly. Many people lack basic analytical skills.

Reason 2: Poor models. Common sense, deadlines and time-management techniques teach us to avoid duplication of effort. Therefore, the reflex action for someone who has just been assigned a new report, proposal, or manual to write is to grab a sample. That would be a good idea, if only the models were adequate. Too often, though, the writer assumes that simply because a document is on file, it's written the way management wants it. Far more often than not, the document has become the department model or form simply because it's there, not because it's necessarily effective, readable, or concise.

Reason 3: Insecurities. We also see a lot of writing by people who:

- Fear they have to use big words and jargon to impress upon their superiors that they know what they're talking about.
- Use vague phrases and generalizations because they don't know what they're talking about, but who feel too insecure to ask for help from the boss.
- Because they can't be creative in their ideas and their work, try to be creative in their *expressions* of worn-out ideas. (They coin new phrases and words and play with sentence structure to add "pizazz," but succeed only in creating grammatical errors and confusion.)

Reason 4: Naive perception about communication's importance. Despite all the studies on how poor writing affects customer reactions and limits career advancement, there are still those who fail to perceive communication, specifically writing, as essential to their job. Some consider it a nice-to-know skill that they may get around to at some point when they are setting goals for self-improvement.

Managers can address all these causes. They can teach their employees to write, to some extent, by simply asking them the right questions or giving the right answers when delegating a writing task. Managers can provide appropriate document models for their subordinates. Managers can allay fears that cause subordinates to write to *impress* rather than to *express*. Finally, managers can assure subordinates that writing skills do count by considering such weaknesses, and strengths, on performance appraisals.

Whatever the reasons for poor writing, you as a manager and your subordinates can improve your writing. Contrary to what those of the inspiration school expound, good, concise, clear writing can be taught.

HOW MUCH DOES YOUR WRITING SKILL AFFECT PROMOTION?

Seventy percent of managers report an increase in the volume of their communications as they move up in the organization, according to researcher Marie Flatley at San Diego State University (*Journal of Business Communications*, Summer 1982).

Managers participating in this survey were asked if they had ever received formal training in writing. Only 4.6 percent of the managers reported no such training. When asked how they viewed the importance of written communication, the overwhelming majority saw it as important. Upper-level managers perceived it as "extremely important" in 62.8 percent of the cases.

A similar study, done by Arthur and Wanda Sharplin, showed that 59.3 percent of managers surveyed among four national firms considered writing skills "very important."

Although these studies can't focus on whether writing skill is a significant consideration in promotion, it only stands to reason that people who are perceived to be weak in this area won't be promoted to positions where communication tasks comprise a large part of the job. But to look at the issue in a positive way, consider what *good* writing skills may mean to your career.

The legendary Alfred P. Sloan, CEO of General Motors from 1923 to 1946, was an exceptional communicator. Presenting his ideas in an early report called "Organization Study," he laid down his concept of decentralization, saying that his great contribution to management would be the concept of running a large, diversified company such as GM through decentralized operations with coordinated control. His rise in the organization was rapid. He began to travel with president Pierre S. du Pont and confer with him on all matters. Then in 1923, when du Pont resigned the presidency, he nominated Sloan to succeed him; the board of directors elected Sloan as president and also elected him chairman of the executive committee. He writes in his autobiography, *My Years with General Motors*:

> In the midst of this welter of thought and attempted action, and a half year before the actual economic and management crisis began, I drafted the "Organization Study" and circulated it unofficially. It became a kind of "best seller" in the corporation all during 1920; I received numerous letters from executives requesting copies of it, so many, in fact, that I found it necessary to reproduce it in quantity.... The new administration was made up of men with very different ideas about business administration. They desired a highly rational and objective mode of operation. The "Organization Study" served the purpose and, as I have related, it was officially adopted, with some revision, as basic corporation policy.... I became president under the auspicious fact that many of my basic views had become the accepted policy of the corporation.

Thus his writing gave him opportunity to prove his other skills.

Lee Iacocca, in his autobiography, also attributes much of his success, as the man who rose to the presidency of the Ford Motor Company and who miraculously revived Chrysler Corporation, to his ability to write:

> The most important thing I learned in school was how to communicate. Miss Raber, our ninth-grade teacher, had us turn in a theme paper of five hundred words every Monday morning. Week in and week out, we had to write that damn paper. By the end of the year, we had learned how to express ourselves in writing.

On the other hand, a lack of good writing skills can severely limit career advancement. The CEO of a small oil-service company brought along a colleague from a former business to assume the vice presidency of his newly formed company. The colleague, who had three college degrees, lasted about two years in the company. "He's brilliant," the CEO explained, "but he can't communicate his ideas." After leaving that company, his credentials got him appointed by the board of directors to a temporary CEO position in a medium-sized company. He was replaced in six weeks. For the three years since that time, he's been trying to persuade investors to join him in advancing a new computer idea—with no results. According to my knowledge of his writing skills, I'd say he probably has had no success because he can't express his ideas well enough in a proposal to gain investors' confidence in his expertise in other areas.

Iacocca learned to write in school; others weren't so fortunate. American business has found that it can't leave to the present educational system and to a few self-motivated students the total process for training in the basics.

IBM spends hundreds of millions of dollars on its educational programs, devoting more dollars to training than any other U.S. organization except the federal government. According to Ray Abuzayyad, president of IBM's General Products Division, speaking at the American Society of Training and Development's national convention, on the average, each IBM employee receives 10 days of education a year. And every manager is *required* to take 40 hours of training each year.

IBM's former chairman, John Opel, who in 1983 co-chaired a task force of 41 governors and business leaders, stated, "If American industry is going to compete with the Japanese, Germans, and the rest of the world, we need engineers, but we also need a workforce that can read and write." (*Business Week*, July 4, 1983.)

Thus IBM, among other corporations, has an Adopt-a-School program that lends equipment to schools and provides IBM employees as teachers. Likewise, International Paper Company publishes and distributes free a series of writing aids entitled "Power of the Printed Word," that covers everything from conciseness to style and spelling.

So if top executives, corporations as a whole, governmental agencies, and educational research groups all agree that writing is essential to conduct business, why do we have writing problems on the job? I can't answer that. When managers insist that they can't afford the time to learn effective skills, I can only ask: How can they afford to continue to miscommunicate and shuffle unnecessary paper?

EFFECTIVE METHODS OF WRITING TRAINING

The following should help you evaluate which is the best method of providing writing training for your organization.

Self-Study Books

Pros:

1. Hardcover texts and paperback workbooks are inexpensive.
2. Learners can work at their own pace and at their own schedule during personal—not company—time.

Cons:

1. Learners must be self-motivated.
2. Some techniques and effects of writing—tone, persuasiveness, directness—can best be learned through feedback from others. Writers must be able to see and hear others' reactions to know if they have accomplished their purpose with a specific writing assignment.

Best use:

1. For isolated learners.
2. For writers with severe weaknesses who cannot find a university or in-house program that covers "the basics" in enough depth for their needs.

Self-Study Computer Software and Videodisc

Pros:

1. Learners can work at their own pace and at their own schedule.

2. Learners can complete courses in about 30 percent less time than with conventional classroom instruction.
3. Computer software is still new enough to be "fun."
4. Learners are actively involved; they must respond to the computer to keep the course moving along.
5. Both learners and developers can control the course content.
6. Computers can provide simulation/drill and practice.

Cons:

1. Learners must be self-motivated to complete the course.
2. Learners must have access to computers.
3. Learners cannot receive feedback on their individual on-the-job writing projects.
4. Courses cannot easily be updated.
5. Development is an expensive investment.

Best use:

1. When computers are readily available and other training programs are available by computer to limit the per-course investment.
2. When isolated learners' travel expenses to other sites would far outweigh the cost of software.

Classroom Programs with In-House Instructor

Pros:

1. Organizations can customize the materials to the specific writing tasks of their audiences.
2. Sessions can be conducted just a few hours each day to suit an audience's particular schedule.
3. In-house instructors can be less expensive than outside consultants. (However, see the third "con" comment.)

Cons:

1. In-house instructors do not always have the credentials or the necessary credibility with the audience.
2. Organizations can become blind to their own weaknesses by not being exposed to more effective and competitive writing styles and formats used by other companies.

3. In-house courses can be quite expensive. Some organizations fail to consider the salary of the in-house trainer, the development time for an effective course (one to two years for a good writing course), and the cost of supplementary materials such as viewgraphs, slides, books, handouts, or films.

Best use:

1. When you have a highly qualified writer as instructor whose credentials will be readily perceived by the audience.
2. When the number of people to train is large enough to offset the investment of developmental time and daily instructor time.

Off-the-Shelf Video Programs

Pros:

1. They are less inexpensive ($2,000-$4,000) than outside consultant fees, in-house course development costs, and travel costs to offsite courses.
2. Quality of the professionally developed film is usually exceptional.
3. Viewing can be scheduled to fit the audience's needs.

Cons:

1. Some sound dull and "canned."
2. Most are generic and may be difficult to tailor to your organization's writing tasks.
3. They can't talk back to learners and answer all their specific questions.
4. They cannot be updated.
5. Learners must have access to video equipment.

Best use:

1. When budget does not allow outside consultant fees.
2. When an in-house trainer does not have adequate credentials to develop and deliver a writing program.
3. When the writing projects of your audience are rather typical of those in other organizations.

Consultant-Led In-House Programs

Pros:

1. Content can be tailored for specific audiences and organizations.
2. Consultants have a broader range and greater depth in the subject due to exposure to many organizations.
3. Consultants usually have the necessary credentials to establish credibility with the audience.
4. Learners usually enjoy an enthusiastic, live trainer more than watching a TV or computer screen.
5. Learners can ask for specific help with their on-the-job writing projects.

Cons:

1. Consultants are expensive.

Best use:

1. When budget allows.
2. When the consultant has superb qualifications.

Consultant-Led Public Programs

Pros:

1. Learners can interact with and get reaction to their writing from those outside their organization.
2. Instructors usually have excellent credentials.

Cons:

1. Learners can't always attend where and when they want to.
2. Tuition and travel costs per learner are expensive compared to in-house courses.
3. Courses are designed to fit audiences of varying needs.

Best use:

1. When you have only a few people to train.
2. When learners are not motivated to use self-study materials.

University-Sponsored Off-Site Courses

Pros:

1. Class sessions are usually longer and scheduled over a longer period, therefore giving the learner time to digest and practice skills between class sessions. The more time, of course, the more topics writers can cover, practice, and master.

Cons:

1. Attendance may be sporadic if learner travels in his or her job or has other personal conflicts during after-work hours.
2. Instructors often lack credentials and credibility with business writers unless they have the means to stay up-to-date on current business writing problems and trends.
3. Programs are generic because they must be geared to varying audiences.

Best Use:

1. When you have only a few writers to train.
2. When writers lack basic academic skills and need more help than a short, on-the-job course can offer.

Whichever way you decide on, train yourself and your staff to write. If you don't, how can you ever hope to cure the paper disease you and your staff may be spreading among yourselves by poor writing and rewriting? How can your company serve its customers and stay competitive with the effective communicators?

12
TALKING
VERSUS
WRITING

RECOMMENDATION: TALK MOST OF YOUR MESSAGES.

WHY DO PEOPLE WRITE?

The Inarticulate

Some people write memos and reports in an attempt to keep from lashing a good idea to death with an untrained tongue. Their ideas frequently get turned down because they sound unproductive, impractical, costly, absurd, or simply vague. When questioned about a minor point, these people don't think well on their feet. Instead, they mumble and mutter an incomplete answer, ending with the disclaimer, "I guess it wasn't such a good idea after all."

So to overcome their lockjaw or lack of confidence, they tend to put everything in writing to ensure accuracy, completeness, and logical progression of ideas. If the results of these "inarticulate" writers, however, were always accurate, complete, and logical, few of their readers would have complaints.

My usual question is: Do you want to read a treatise on why lockers in the company-sponsored recreational facility should be repainted blue? Some subjects aren't worth the paper on which they're printed.

133

The Easily Intimidated

Many have learned that the boss's or co-workers' open-door policy is far from it. Although the door may be indeed open, there's a protective secretary who halts passersby as they attempt to enter, or the phone's equipped with an answering machine that asks you to leave a message rather than interrupt. Some people take these obstacles seriously.

Those who are good time managers, of course, have periods in which they do not want to be disturbed, and certainly such times should be respected.

The problem is that some people *never* feel comfortable about intruding upon someone else's time—no matter how lavishly and wastefully that time is being spent. These are the people who tiptoe up to an office door and hear the person inside talking to a secretary about a golf game and, rather than ask for a few minutes to give some information, wander off with "I guess I can come back when he's not busy."

Some would-be writers don't realize that "she can't be interrupted now" means *now*, not always.

The Suspicious

Others write rather than talk because they don't or can't trust. They're afraid their statistics may be taken out of context or otherwise misused or misconstrued. They're afraid the boss will not understand how much work has gone into a project unless they produce reams of evidence. They want all their ideas recorded so as to be sure to get sole credit for them.

They write memos to the file to document all their accomplishments in case someone says they aren't doing their job or tries to lay blame for a failure at their feet. They document all conversations to confirm details that may come back to haunt them later or may be useful to hold someone to the truth.

They don't trust computers or any electronic equipment; therefore, they print out and store in at least four places hard copies of everything.

The Frustrated Artists

Obviously, we have some frustrated artists in the business world, a minority sect who like to write—novels, poems, book reviews, treatises on the state of the economy to be published on the Op-ed page of their local newspapers. Invariably in a workshop of 15 participants during the course of our two to four days, at least one or two participants whisper to me in hushed tones their hidden ambition to break into published print.

The "Authorized"

Some people write because they think anything official has to be in writing. Therefore, as the person "authorized" to take charge of the situation, they put all their edicts in writing so they get the appropriate attention. Some writers even carry this concept a little further and equate "official" and "authorized" with "tone." Rather than say, "As we discussed last week...," they write "Pursuant to our discussion last week...," in an attempt to make their documents sound official, whatever that is.

No one has told these voluminous writers that if they are conducting the business their company has authorized them to conduct, their *talk* is official for all internal purposes. (If that's not the case in your particular organization, it should be. Writing is not the only way to get official things done.)

WHEN TO TALK

Talk When You Want Immediate Feedback

Waiting builds frustration. The bigger the organization or the department, the longer the usual wait for an answer. Take the initiative in deciding what can wait for an answer and what should be taken care of immediately. Trust your judgment about adverse effects of delay; and eventually, if you're right most of the time, the boss or co-worker will become more trusting of your need-to-know without the red tape.

Talk When You Want to See the Reaction to Your Message

On occasion, it's important for you to see what effect your message has on the other person. What does the body language convey? Disappointment? Disapproval? Resignation? Acceptance? Wait-and-see?

Doubt? Mild hope? Enthusiasm? Your next action, reaction or interpretation perhaps will turn what you see and understand rather than on what you read from the other person.

Talk When You Have to Negotiate

Why write when half of what you say will have to be changed in later negotiations? I've spent months in contract negotiations simply because both parties insisted on putting their offers in writing rather than talking. Shuffling paragraphs that have been added, amended, qualified, and initialed certainly takes more time than talking through the give-and-take and then drafting the contract. (Yes, I know about the bird-in-hand negotiating approach.)

But don't limit your thinking necessarily to formal contracts. Employees negotiate all sorts of things: Which projects am I assigned? What is the real due date on this, and how long a grace period do I have? Which is worth more to me at my next performance review—a 7 percent increase or paid tuition to three professional development courses at the university? If I add 10 more people to the luncheon guest list, will they cut the price of the lunch by $3 a person?

Talk is by far the cheapest and most effective method for negotiating situations such as the above.

Talk When You Need to Listen to the Other Person

Talk, although it may start out as a weak monologue, will often become more effective when it turns to a dialogue. Sometimes people need to start talking just so they are forced to listen—and to give answers—to the other's needs, interests, concerns, and questions.

We would have much better written reports if writers were forced to listen to the questions their readers have as they plow through the pages of a rough draft. Salespeople know that before they ever tell customers how they can meet the customers' needs, they themselves have to listen to the wants and questions of their buyers. Unfortunately, not all salespeople know the value of listening. Perhaps that is why so many rejected people end their selling careers early.

The same is true of many employees who write their ideas, information, status reports and objectives. They never check to see if anybody's listening—or reading, that is.

Talk When You Need to Persuade the Disinterested

People find it harder to say no to a flesh-and-blood face or to a telephone voice than they do to a piece of paper. That's why employment counselor Richard Bolles, author of the bestseller *What Color Is Your Parachute?*, among other career consultants, insists that you do almost anything to talk to prospective employers rather than write or drop a resume in the mail; you have a much better chance of getting your foot in the door with a voice rather than with pen and paper.

The same is true in most ventures. Consider fundraising. Which strategy gets the best result: the direct-mail appeal or the personal appointment?

When you need to sell a boss on a solution to a problem, talk to him or her first. Then when you get as far as a fair hearing, switch tactics to paper to prove that you have thoroughly evaluated the idea or solution to all logical ends.

Talk When What You Have to Say Will Be Incredibly Boring to Read

Comedians know that very funny stories often die on paper. Effective speakers know that to read a speech is to have supreme confidence in your subject's power to hold the audience's attention. If your reports, policy statements, proposals, or memos aren't inherently interesting, then don't bore your audience to death.

Talk your report, your problem, your proposal, your solution and give it a fighting chance for survival. Otherwise, your written document may be shoved to the side until there's absolutely no other excuse to avoid reading it.

When you can sum up your work or the status of a customer account in 15 seconds, why write?

Talk When You Need to Give Mild Reprimands

Reprimanding face to face allows the listener the courtesy of privacy, and therefore, dignity. Anytime a document is written, the intended audience is not the only party who knows the document's content. Consider the clerk who typed the memo, the passersby who looked over her shoulder and/or typewriter while she worked, the coworker who saw the longhand draft on your desk. There's rarely such a thing as a private internal document.

So why the concern for privacy? Privacy often defuses the need for retaliation—whether it be a sulk, a verbal retort, the sabotage of a project, or a stinging written reply. Importantly, when one feels deserving of the reprimand and is allowed to lick one's wounds in private, there's no need for a public response from the spectators.

A third reason is the recovery rate. Spoken words can be easily forgotten or interpreted and reinterpreted in a better light. They can be tempered with body language and a supportive smile. Gradually, the hearer's memory begins to fade on exactly what was said. And as the listener gains perspective, he or she reinterprets in such a way as to focus on the solution or desired action. On the other hand, written messages are often read and reread until they gradually take on ominous, between-the-line meanings that the writer never intended.

To many people, what you put in writing is an event, the unusual, a turning point of major consequence. If your reprimand is *not* of such grave significance, do it face to face.

Formal reprimands or dismissals, of course, need to be documented for possible legal repercussions.

Talk When "How You Say It" Is As Important as "What" You Say

Written words are flat. They often don't appropriately convey the tone or seriousness of their message. Many people who have first been persuaded with talk have become dissuaded when they saw "the whole" in black print on white paper. Customers particularly shy away from the paperwork part of buying. They like to own, not to buy.

Additionally, bad news doesn't seem quite so bad when spoken in an optimistic, upbeat tone. Support, commitment to a project or a person, and willingness to compromise can best be conveyed through inflection, a lifted eyebrow, an upturned mouth, or a shrug of the shoulder. Paper conveys only one-dimensional words.

Talk When You Don't Want Your Words Coming Back to Burn You

Many employees use an angry memo or letter as the first match to burn the bridge with and live to regret the fire. Resignation letters and replies to performance appraisals perhaps lead the list of regrets.

But even the good news—the promises and the pluses—may set a fire under some employee who, in his or her own mind, holds you to a written promise that later you may have lost the power or resources to deliver on. Richard Nixon and—if we are to believe Lee Iacocca—Henry Ford III learned to regret and finally to destroy writing that at best confuses and at worst compounds later decisions and responsibilities.

Ask yourself if you are willing to take the risk that putting something in writing may bring. If the stakes are high and you want to claim credit for your part in a project whatever the outcome, write it. But if the stakes are not so high, and you won't relish blame, talk your part and take your chances on who remembers your contributions.

WHEN TO WRITE

Write to Stay Out of Court

Document plans or discussions that may be the basis for legal action. Specifically, put in writing poor performance appraisals, warnings about dismissal, and actual dismissal notices. Record agreements that involve large sums of money. I'm not so naive as to think we can still do all business on a handshake. But I do think handshakes carry a lot more weight than the more suspicious among us think.

Write to Persuade When You Have a Hostile Audience

If you are fairly certain that a spoken message will get an immediate "no" because your listener is known for brash, impulsive responses, then you may decide to write to give him or her time to evaluate in a more thorough manner.

Writing is more effective than talking when the other person will have to lose face to accept your message. He or she may need recuperation time to identify, and practice reciting, reasons for acceptance of your message: "In light of other information of which I was unaware...," "In light of the new turn of events last week ...," "In light of options I have been considering on my own..." or "Because of other reasons I'm not at liberty to discuss..." Allow your reader whatever face-saving ploys he or she needs to agree with and/or accept your message.

The written message also gives the reader time to think and calculate before giving an unfavorable answer or reaction.

Write to Praise

For the same reasons you reprimand in private, face to face, you should praise in public. If you don't have a regular monthly, quarterly, or annual hoopla meeting to orally commend your people, then the next-best method of commendation is writing and circulating your praise. Praise can best and, sometimes, only be enjoyed when shared. For some people, the public record that elicits recognition from peers is the primary sweetener in the commendation or thank-you message.

When you go on record with your praise, you motivate a specific employee, but your message may also motivate other readers to greater achievements for your attention. An added benefit of praising in public by writing is that it's much more difficult for the one praised to backtrack and slip into a malaise of mediocrity with everyone watching.

Write to Give Complex Information

Although the human brain is perhaps the most marvelous of all computers, most of us have trouble keeping it on-line all the time. Therefore, when the message is complex, we may need to enter data slowly in an organized pattern—one much more organized than the way most of us speak. The written message, then, allows us to enter data slowly, analyze it, and recall it to the mind's screen again and again until we can understand and retrieve the information in usable form.

Remember, however, that complex information should not be synonymous with boring information.

If the complex information happens to be details about how to run a machine, specifications for placing a billion-dollar order, or personnel data, make it usable. If the information will be referred to over a long period of time for varying details, arrange the message in appropriate formats for easy skimming of specifics. That is, use numerous headings and make them informative; prefer lists to long paragraphs, provide extensive indexes; and include a table of contents.

Write to Think

Some employees write as an aid to thinking, although a time-consuming aid it is. In fact, Lee Iacocca in his autobiography insists that writing down a good idea is the best way to think it through. You can get away with all kinds of vagueness and with generalities and handle all obstacles and objections when talking. But when you have to come up with the 1, 2, 3's and furthermore's you have to be on solid ground.

Fiction and nonfiction authors are often admonished by their peers: If you talk it, you won't ever write it. Talking dissipates the emotional energy that may otherwise spur you on to thinking creatively about, and communicating a message to, a bigger audience. Additionally, by talking, thinkers frequently get their intrapreneurial ideas shot down before they've really had time to let them germinate; as a result, the author of the idea tends to discard it without even trying to overcome the face-to-face objections and discouragement.

"Write it, don't talk it" is good advice for authors whose aim is to get published and paid. It's also good advice for business.

But employees tend to do just the opposite—with poor results. They tend to talk about their creative ideas to see what others think before investing the time to put the ideas in writing. Therefore, many good ideas get shot down before they've had a chance to catch on. And, to top it off, these same employees tend to write about the routine information—perhaps because it's incredibly boring to would-be listeners and because talkers of routine messages soon lose their audience.

Whatever the reasons, business writers should *write* the creative and *talk* the routine messages.

13

ELECTRONIC

INFORMATION

RECOMMENDATION: PASS ON INFORMATION
ELECTRONICALLY, WHEN YOU CAN, RATHER
THAN BY PAPER—PARTICULARLY INFORMATION
THAT BECOMES OBSOLETE ALMOST AS SOON AS
IT BECOMES HARD COPY.

"The biggest problem facing American business today is that most managers have too much information. It dazzles them, and they don't know what to do with it all," writes Lee Iacocca in his autobiography.

Not a new idea. Iaccoca simply echoed Goethe (1810): "The modern age has a false sense of superiority because of the great mass of data at its disposal, but the valid criterion of distinction is rather the extent to which man knows how to form and master the material at his command."

Two-thirds of a manager's time is spent in passing information internally within the organization, estimates Paul Strassman, systems specialist and former vice president at Xerox, in his 1985 book, *Information Payoff: The Transformation of Work in the Electronic Age.* Of course, most of that information-passing could be done better by computer. Strassman predicts that the role of the middle manager as information gatherer and supplier will diminish rapidly and that this middle manager will take on more and more of the decision-making authority and tasks of the senior manager. In turn, the top executives will be left to strategic planning and brainstorming new intrapreneurial ventures.

But you can bet that most of the information now falling in a deluge upon these managers is hard copy—the result of electronic information messaging. In fact, many managers panic when someone talks about doing away with paper. They think somehow that that person is suggesting they give up all the statistics so readily available to them—the information they have come to consider synonymous with power and protection.

Where is all the information coming from? Government and technology. It seems that the government grants money to just anybody to study just about anything; and such institutions and agencies with such grants turn out reams of research data.

Retired Colonel Leonard S. Lee, business records management expert in charge of buying and implementing the RAM2 program that automated approximately 800,000 Army personnel records, writes in *Records Management Quarterly* (April 1982)

> The magnitude/costs involving just U.S. Federal Government operations are mind-boggling. Total records holdings now exceed 265 billion documents, are stored in 20 (to 30) million cubic feet of space, and 30 billion new items of information are prepared annually by states, local governments and individuals (excluding corporate inputs). Paperwork costs total over $100 billion yearly, including demands upon American businesses that add up to $40 million (an average of $500 for every person in the United States).

In addition to what the government funds and gathers on its own, technology has made it possible to put isolated facts into computers and come up with a mixture suitable for just about any purpose or interpretation. Experts tell us that information in the world is doubling about every six years, and there's no sign of a reverse in this trend. Yes, information is power.

But managers today must stop equating information with paper and protection. As far as information protection goes, microfilm records have been ruled acceptable in our courts: the Uniform Photography Act, the Best Evidence Rule, and Business Records Exception to Hearsay.

And paper itself? For example, incoming mail? It's only one form of information, and information should be thought of in many different ways. For instance, consider cost and control. Should you have all the information you need for various decisions in-house or should you buy it outside through database hookups? You can buy on-line data-based research, microfiche, videos, telephone messages, or bound paper reports that summarize the computer printouts. You must, of course, determine the source, accuracy and timeliness of the information gathered.

Now that you know that I'm not speaking of giving up information altogether (but only the hard copy of it that your organization generates), let's talk about "why" electronics rather than paper.

WHY NOT PAPER?

Costs

Manufacturers of filing apparatus report that the average company wastes 65 cents of every dollar for paper records processing and filing operations.

Records-management experts estimate that the average company stores up to 70 percent more paper than necessary and never even refers to 85-90 percent of all documents after they're filed. (The discrepancy in the 70 percent of unnecessary paper and the 85-90 percent of paper never again retrieved refers to those records the government requires business to keep, but which are not needed by the company itself.) And 45 percent of all storage space is occupied by duplicate copies!

Col. Leonard Lee goes on to estimate that businesses average about 18,000 documents and four file drawers for each white-collar employee. What's more, this storage problem increases by about 4,000 pages per employee per year.

Automation of this information-processing and storage function can reduce annual operating costs by 30 percent, a conservative figure.

Let's get more specific. Following are some figures from companies using various forms of electronic communication:

Corning Glass Works: Information services division managers used a "soft" example of eliminating one memo a day per user. A conservative 10 percent of a subscriber base of 2,000 was used in determining a savings of $405,000 annually. "Hard" cost savings of reduced telephone call charges amounted to $51,000 annually. (Assumptions: 50 cents per minute and reduction of two minutes per call for 10 percent of 2,000 users.) (*The Office Magazine*, August 1984)

Westinghouse: Westinghouse calculated a $620,000 annual savings on internal communications among 2,000 users. (*Speech Technology*, Aug-Sept 1984, *Communication News*, May 1982)

Ford Motor Company: In 1983 Ford launched two pilot programs involving 480 employees. The company realized a savings of over $700,000 during the test period. (*Speech Technology*, Aug-Sept 1984)

Hercules Inc.: Ross O. Watson, vice president for information resources, estimates that their electronic mail system has saved $3 million annually in employees' time. Their satellite system has helped save more than $1.5 million a year in time and travel and expenses. They have trimmed 1,800 jobs, or 6.6 per cent of their work force, and eliminated a "half a dozen" layers of management. (*Business Week*, October 8, 1984)

Slower Retrieval

Cost is not only measured in dollars and cents but also in inadequate customer service and dwindling business traceable directly to slower retrieval of records and to what customers perceive as inattention to their needs and requests. Companies who deal with excessive paperwork, such as banks, brokerage houses, and insurance companies, say they have improved customer satisfaction tremendously by computerizing their records. Clerks can call a customer's account to the screen, answer questions, print out requested information, update records, and correct errors—all almost immediately.

With paper records, the clerk usually responds with a "hold the line" (which customers sometimes do for up to 10 minutes) and then makes a trip to the file cabinet. If the document is not misfiled (which happens 3 percent of the time) and if someone else hasn't pulled the record for other reasons, the clerk can get back to the customer rather quickly—perhaps as fast as the competition can. To stay *ahead* of the competition, you need quicker access than paper records provide.

Why rush to compile information when you and your clients can't get to it?

Continuous Updating

Paper records, such as policy statements, procedures, desk manuals, and the like are outdated almost as soon as they are turned into hard copy. Employees can seldom trust them to be accurate. Therefore, after they look up the item in question, they have to call the person responsible for the paper document and double-check the information. And even if your organization or department prides itself on up-to-date manuals, consider the clerical time spent in adding updated pages to binder copies and the printer costs involved in reduplicating and rebinding such records.

Updates via computer require only a fraction of the above effort.

HOW TO USE THE LATEST TECHNOLOGY TO PASS ON INFORMATION

Electronic Text Messages and Voice Mailboxes

Eliminating telephone tag and short memos. Studies show that only one in four business calls are completed on the first attempt. If you've ever played telephone tag, you know that electronically recorded messages reduce frustration, as well as get your messages to you as accurately as, or more so than, paper. When receptionists take phone messages, you may later notice that some things get lost in translation. You may also experience the delay and frustration of not knowing when and if the messages (calls and memos) you send are ever passed on to the intended audience.

Ensuring accuracy and receipt. With electronic text and voice messages, you can record your message yourself, to ensure accuracy, and know that at the earliest possible moment the receiver will punch in his or her code and get your information or question—whether he or she comes into the home office at midnight or visits a branch office in Kalamazoo. And with voice messaging, the tone is right when you speak your message yourself—no more implications missed because the words didn't match the intended inflection. In fact, with the return-receipt feature, the sender can find out who has received his or her message and who hasn't.

Scheduling meetings and projects. Many organizations also use electronic means for scheduling meetings and coordinating project due dates. If you've ever had your secretary call five people and get them to agree to attend a Friday morning meeting and then found the sixth person called cannot attend, you know the time involved in retracking the first five and starting over again: "Now what time did you say you had open on Tuesday? George can attend only after 3:00, whatever day we pick." Instead, the electronic meeting schedule feature checks everyone's calendar and presents the scheduler with the possible choices for those who must attend—a much more efficient system and one that can't be manipulated by the most vocal of the attendees.

And, of course, the value of having the "right people" at meetings cannot be overestimated.

Transmitting the routine administrative details for wide distribution. Administrative people can make all sorts of routine announcements, from instruction about training classes to new products. They enter a few key strokes and send the message simultaneously to a long list of people. And, with the return-receipt feature—unlike the memo-reading game—the sender can find out who has received the message and who hasn't.

Keeping in touch on the road. Another benefit to traveling business people is the opportunity, with voice messaging, to call in last-minute changes on their itineraries or orders. When such records have to be mailed, they are outdated almost by the time they are received at headquarters.

Minimizing isolation. For those who travel much of the time, those whose business isolates them at distant sites, or those who work strange hours, electronic messages are a morale booster. When they're on the road, these travelers can call in and pick up and leave messages wherever they are—no matter what time zone in the United States or abroad.

Reducing the time and charges for chit-chat. Whether by electronic text or voice messaging, the sender increases productivity by eliminating time spent in chit-chat that normally goes with face-to-face discussions or conversation calls. Studies show that the sender makes about five voice-message calls in the same time normally spent on one regular call. When you are at a busy airport, there's no waiting on hold and no need to spell out everything for the message-taker. Those few extra minutes from an airport phone can cross off a great deal more paperwork from the to-do list. Of course, making faster calls reduces long-distance charges. Additionally, callers can send voice messages during off-peak hours at lower rates even when the office closes at five.

Allowing better time management. Electronic message senders and receivers can control their own time and minimize interruptions. They aren't harassed by a ringing phone; instead, when they finish a project and schedule a break, they can pick up their messages and answer them at a convenient time.

Increasing response time to customers. If immediate response time to customers is essential, as with insurance companies, brokerage houses, banks, and the like, then electronic messages allow you to service your accounts in a way that lets customers know you appreciate their business. When you give them the number and code to your special equipment and let them leave you messages, they feel as if you're giving them special attention—much like the obstetrician who gives the expectant patient his or her unlisted phone number.

Eliminating message-taking staff. All of the above is to imply, of course, that if you record your own messages by terminal or telephone, you can eliminate the need for several clerical employees throughout the organization. And almost any manager with a secretary can eliminate the need for hiring a "temporary" while the permanent secretary or receptionist is on vacation or out of the office ill. Primarily, all a "temp" does is to answer the phone and record messages. If that need is met by voice mail, the manager can cut the cost of such help from the budget.

So, for all these benefits, how long does it take before the average learner is able to use the system? Twenty to thirty minutes. (If it takes longer than that, the user really doesn't want to learn.) At what cost? Depending on the number of users, from $15,000 to over $500,000. Small companies that cannot afford to buy their own system can use service bureaus, which buy large systems and resell the voice messaging service. Investigate your options.

Videoconferencing and Audioconferencing

Consider teleconferencing for coordinating efforts among your decentralized work groups, for training employees, and for single-event purposes. The list of organizations using electronic communications goes on and on, growing with each addition of a new feature and each reduction in the price of equipment.

Uses generally fall into one of several applications: new-product or new-service announcements, press conferences, teaching seminars, specialist expertise to or from a remote site, and general employee meetings.

Videoconferencing and audioconferencing, of course, must take place in real time; that is, participants must schedule time to be on-line simultaneously. But electronic meetings do not take anywhere near the amount of time in-person meetings require (30 to 70 percent of a manager's day according to research findings).

Remember that not every kind of information exchange needs the personal touch. By some estimates, nearly 20 percent of all business trips can be eliminated by teleconferencing. Teleconferencing allows participants to remain on the job except for the actual on-line time, eliminating human downtime in getting to and from a meeting. Not only time but also other travel costs can be deducted from the usual meeting method. Thus, people who otherwise would not be able to "attend" a meeting because of traveling expense or schedule conflicts can tune into the electronic information exchange. (However, travel is still a perk and some employees will always prefer getting on a plane to sitting down to a terminal.)

Additionally, because of the formality and the greater focus and participation of each member, discussion stays on target. The business that may take three hours around a conference table may take only 15 minutes electronically.

Other benefits include the fact that a record is kept of all entered comments. This record can be accessed by entering an author's name, date, and key words. Also, the shy people who rarely speak in face-to-face meetings are often more "vocal" in entering their comments, facts, statistics, and details to the record. In fact, these electronic meetings limit those who would try to monopolize the time in a face-to-face meeting. Additionally, they who wish to do so may enter their comments anonymously—possibly a boon to honesty. Another benefit is that the responses these anonymous comments bring cannot be dismissed as "personality differences" by those who may want to downplay objections.

Yet another benefit is that participants have time to think before they respond to others' comments—unlike in a face-to-face discussion where most reactions are off the cuff and, unfortunately, not always well thought out.

Businesses use teleconferencing primarily for strictly routine information exchange, such as sales, statistics, budgeting, forecasting, surveying. They find it a useful way to brainstorm solutions to problems that require expertise from numerous conference members. The teleconference also brings together daily reports from people who are separated geographically, such as patrolmen on duty in different parts of the country or branch officers reporting sales receipts deposited for the day.

Try getting on-line rather than on paper or on a plane. With a little thought, you can overcome "soft" obstacles in implementing the system—technophobia, the organizational culture ("but we've always..."), and the social ("But I like to 'chew the fat' awhile") reactions to electronic communication.

Micrographics

There are six generic microforms: updatables (microfiche and microfilm jackets), traditional microfiche, computer output microfilm (COM), ultrafiche and ultrastrip, aperture cards, and roll film. Each has its advantages and disadvantages, and this discussion will not attempt to tell you which will meet your needs best; you can call in several vendors to do that.

But here are the basic advantages of a micrographics system:

1. Annual operating costs can be reduced by at least 30 percent.
2. Film records can be located faster than paper records. The average retrieval time for a paper document is three to five minutes. Automated retrieval is 25 percent to several hundred percent faster and film records are less vulnerable to misfiling.
3. Microfilm is physically more manageable. It's easier to transport four thin microfiche sheets than to carry armsful of the equivalent information on paper. Mailing costs are reduced accordingly.
4. Microfilm is a convenient way to keep related facts together on one thin sheet for easy review.
5. Security (against loss, misuse, theft) is more efficient because of the manageable size and fewer handlers. Also, files are difficult, if not impossible, to alter.
6. Microfilm saves space, requiring only 2 to 10 percent of the storage space necessary for paper documents. You also save on processing costs involved in sorting, filing, retrieving, and refiling. (Figure your rent per square foot and multiply by the number of your filing cabinets to get a good idea of the savings with microfiche storage.)

Raymond Sutcliffe, general manager at Eastman Kodak, writing in *The Office*, April 1981, says that 78 percent of Kodak's computer reporting is computer output to microfilm. They have reduced costs in excess of $5 million a year by using film instead of paper for computer output.

Hire an Information Manager

Information is without value if it can't be accessed when needed. That sounds like an obvious idea, but organizations continue to file information they can't find later and to pay for information they can't interpret.

Make information management a primary, dynamic force in your organization by coordinating information organizationally rather than by duplicating effort from department to department or division to division. Information gathering and managing can't be a haphazard process.

But, as Robert Kalthoff and Leonard Lee note, citing the Three Mile Island nuclear power plant incident as a prime example, we are having quite some difficulty in doing just that—in harnessing and mastering our information. The report on the mock-up of the Three Mile Island accident revealed that the operators had so much information coming in from so many sources in so many different forms at such a frequency that they could not turn the information to real benefit in making their split-second decisions.

Information is becoming an organization's primary asset, and retrieval of the right information at the right time is critical to success. Accidents and catastrophes aside, in these days of high interest rates, getting information a few days faster to help managers make a decision a few days sooner can mean the difference between leading the pack and following the pack. Star managers learn to access the available information, whether to spot trends and develop opportunities or to cut losses before the ordinary managers find out "who's writing the report."

In addition to reducing the cost of paper-records handling, an information manager who can keep on-line information at everyone's fingertips boosts morale. People don't have to wait a week to get information they need immediately. And those who don't like to handle the routine, drudge paperwork (who does?) appreciate having the information manager keep policy, procedures, accounts, or inventory up to date for them.

In other words, passing information along electronically rather than with paper can revolutionize your role in the workforce and free you to take on more and more profitable projects for your organization. Let those who aren't quite so ambitious push paper.

14
OUT-GOING
RESPONSES

RECOMMENDATION: DON'T PROCRASTINATE ON PAPER
COMING INTO YOUR OFFICE. TAKE ACTION AT ONCE
AND SEND THE INFORMATION (NOT ADDITIONAL
PAPER) OUT AGAIN.

WHY?—TIME AND MONEY

Earlier I mentioned that records-management experts estimate that 45 percent of all papers filed are *duplicate* copies. And 85-90 percent of all papers that you keep are never referred to once they get into the files. The storage and maintenance of those duplicates and unnecessarily kept originals costs you about $2,160 per four-drawer file per year.

Consider what those files cost you in thinking, or analytical, time. When you fail to take action on what comes into your office, you double your handling time; when you lay something aside to think about it or to take care of it when you have more time, invariably you read the document twice.

Let's get more specific about the cost of your reading load: According to my survey of professionals, middle managers, and senior managers, they spend 10 to 16 hours each week reading. Dr. Phyllis Miller, president of Reading Development Seminars, has collected information through a study done at Sperry Univac among both technical and managerial people. This study showed that on the average, people in both lower levels and higher levels spend 15 to 20 hours each week in work-related reading, roughly one-third to one-half their work week. If we use one-third as a conservative average, the cost of the reading load of the $70,000 (plus 30 percent for benefits) senior manager amounts to $33,333 annually.

Isn't the *necessary* paperwork and reading expensive enough? Why double that time by reading everything twice—when it arrives on your desk and again later when you decide to respond?

But, some will argue, if I lay the paper aside until I get more details or information, I can respond more appropriately. Study after study reveals that such is not the case. In the vast majority of situations, the reader has as much information for a decision or an answer on first handling of the paper as on second and subsequent handlings.

The time lost in retrieving the paper either from your desk or from the files should also be considered in your cost of handling out-going responses. Remember, too, that 3 percent of all documents will be misfiled, thereby increasing the retrieval time.

So keep that paper moving. Here's how.

READ FASTER AND WITH PURPOSE

Most documents fall into several general categories: technical reports, proposals, data information sheets and listings, manuals, correspondence. These documents cannot be read and processed in the same way.

When you begin to read a document, look at its purpose. A glance at a good subject line should tell you what it's all about. Without this purpose, you will have to read through the details twice to comprehend what the writer is trying to tell you and what he or she wants you to do. If the incoming document starts with the background and details and then builds a case before getting to the punchline, you almost always will have to read the document a second time to reprocess the details with the purpose (or expected action from you) in mind.

If the MADE format suggested in Chapter 7 is adopted company-wide, then you will find the message and action statements at the very beginning of the document. When that's the case, frequently you will not have to read the document in its entirety. Your time and specific interests will dictate how much or how little you need to read to grasp the key information.

If the writer has chosen some less effective arrangement, try to identify what arrangement that is and go immediately to the purpose or bottom-line message (frequently marked "Conclusions and Recommendations"). There you'll find what and why you should be reading and what action you need to take on the paper you've received. Then go back to the beginning of the document and read any details you may need.

If you find you need more details, look at the overall document structure to highlight key points in your mind; note the headings, captions under tables, charts, graphs, illustrations, then first sentences of each section and first sentences of each paragraph. This spot reading should give you the gist of the information and also provide the structure, or memory pegs, on which to hang key points.

Reading with pen in hand is also a good idea. Mark key ideas, facts, figures, and names for ease in relocating them later.

If you trust the work of the person writing to you, rarely should you have to read an entire document to make a decision, to take the appropriate action, or to be sufficiently informed. Subordinates who will actually work the plan will get into the specific details of the document.

SCHEDULE UNINTERRUPTED READING TIME

Reading is not something to work into and around your other tasks. Although you should never be caught in a waiting line or at the dentist's waiting room without a reading file, avoid trying to take care of major reading projects in that manner. Grabbing snatches of time is fine for light reading, but save the complex material for concentrated attention. In fact, have your secretary prepare two reading files: must reading (reports, correspondence) and light reading (professional articles, nice-to-know updates).

HAVE YOUR SECRETARY PREREAD

Ask your secretary to use a pen to highlight key facts, or questions to be answered, in your incoming correspondence. A secretary can be valuable by reading all "FYI" documents, circulars, advertisements, professional journal articles, and the like. Let her read in detail and highlight what she thinks will be of interest to you. (As you teach her more about your business and responsibilities, she can become much more proficient in highlighting items of interest.) Also, she can supply, in the margins, pertinent information from other files—information that you may need to make an immediate decision on or response to the reading material.

Example: Incoming correspondence invites you to attend a professional conference June 6-9. Secretary highlights that sentence and in the margin adds her own note: "Conflict with Phoenix management meeting on June 7-8."

Example: Incoming correspondence asks you to make a donation to a favorite charity. Secretary highlights that sentence and notes in the margin: "You contributed $200 last year on April 6."

Example: Incoming memo asks you what you've done about customer complaints on XYZ product. Secretary highlights that sentence and related questions, attaches related letters and memos from that complaining customer, and adds note in the margin: "You have granted a $350 refund to both customers involved. You had also asked that both customers respond to your questionnaire by June 2, but only Mr. Jones has returned it."

Such prereading by the secretary should cut your reading and response time considerably.

GET OFF OTHERS' DISTRIBUTION LISTS

Many of the people who send you courtesy copies can give you absolutely no reason to read—much less respond—to their information. So when you get copies of routine reports or policy statements that you have no use for, return them to the sender with a note saying "thanks, but no thanks." Explain that you are purging your reading and storage files of nonessential information and that you'll let them know if you ever have a further need for information contained in the report.

A phone call to the secretary who prepared the distribution list should be equally effective and fast in getting your name removed from others' lists.

For those reports that you do need, find out if your copy is simply a duplicate of one that another person in your department keeps. If several in your area are getting copies of the same report, you don't need to get and/or save all of those copies.

USE APPROVAL LINES

Ask your staff to prepare incoming documents as suggested in Chapter 3. That is, have them provide an approval line at the bottom of the page for your signature (your full name and title typed underneath it), along with a date line. Then all you have to do to approve what they've asked is to sign and return the approved document to them or to send it on up the chain to the next person who will need to be informed or will need to take action.

Signing your name is a lot quicker than writing a complete letter or memo that basically says, "I agree." In addition to saving you time, the approval line has the other benefits mentioned earlier in Chapter 3: fewer delays, ownership and pride of writer, better copy, elimination of the write/edit/rewrite syndrome.

What if you disapprove of the idea or project and don't want to send the document up the ladder? Then, you can write your comments in the margin, dictate a "no" response, or phone or call a meeting with the originator of the document to discuss changes.

UNCLUTTER YOUR DESK SO YOU KNOW WHAT'S THERE TO SEND OUT

Organized people respond faster than others to their messages. If, after reading a good time-management book, you can't organize yourself and your work, at least get a secretary or assistant who can.

Don't procrastinate. If the written project seems insurmountable, edge up on the task. Break the task into small steps and force yourself to accomplish a little at a time. Make two or three phone calls to get information on its way to you, outline the key points you want to make, locate a diagram or specification sheet in the files. Then, when all the preliminary writing steps are completed, prepare a first draft. Small step by small step, the writing project will edge toward completion.

If you procrastinate because you can't say no, then learn how to say it. Delay usually builds false expectations in the minds of those who are waiting on an answer and compounds the disappointment and difficulty your reader experiences from your negative response. When your "no" is inevitable, get it over with.

DECIDE HOW FORMAL THE PAPER HAS TO BE

Writing does characterize the writer; errors and sloppy paperwork from your office can destroy your credibility on other matters. But I'm not specifying mistakes and illegibility; I'm talking about formality and informality.

Eighty to 90 percent of most company correspondence is internal. And that means that most of your documents can be less formal than the 10-20 percent going outside your organization.

With most internal documents, informality should be the rule. Prefer the timely response to the formally typed one. And if you absolutely must keep a copy of the incoming document and your response to it, simply copy that document with your added notations.

Write your comments in the margins. Beside the questions the writer has asked, note your answers. Poor handwriting is hardly a problem worth worrying about when you're writing only a word or phrase and when the question it answers is plainly in sight in typescript.

Use rubber stamps. If you deal with the routine, stamp an approval line, a date of receipt, a date of processing, or whatever on the original and send the document on its way.

And don't rule out rubber stamps for longer, more specific messages such as the following I've seen used lately:

> Please do not send this completed form to our office. Instead it should be forwarded to the Texas Employment Commission at ...

> Your payment has been received and recorded. Thank you for your prompt attention to the outstanding balance. We look forward to processing further orders from you.

Whatever the standard message that you seem to be sending day after day, document after document, consider a stamp, particularly on internal documents.

Use a pen and "buck" slip. Do you have to type a response? If the message is too long to write in the margin of the original, write a quick note on a "buck" slip and keep the paper moving to its destination.

Type it yourself if it doesn't have to be perfect. If you really are one of the few whose handwriting is so illegible that the reader can't decipher it, type it on your own typewriter or word processor. Anyone with minimal keyboard skills should be able to type a sentence more quickly than explaining to a secretary what she should say in her typed note, and then rereading, approving, and signing her typed note. Try it and see.

Only if you decide that your outgoing response should be formal, should you spend the extra time to have your secretary type it. Formal reports, meeting minutes, contracts, newsletters, and external correspondence should be typed. All formal and all out-going documents such as these deserve the time they require to prepare.

DICTATE

When you must prepare a formal response—a letter, a report, a contract, a fact sheet—dictate.

The average person writes about 20-30 words per minute by longhand. The average person talks about 150-180 words per minute. Therefore, you can understand why dictating longer documents is much faster than writing them by hand and then having the secretary type them.

Another advantage of dictating, other than speed, is a more conversational tone. Those who tediously write and revise by longhand frequently find they have two "voices": a writing voice and a talking voice. Their writing voice usually sounds stuffy and formal compared to their talking voice. Dictation helps writers make their documents sound as conversational and friendly as they do in person.

When dictating, follow the same rules to plan your document as the thinking steps given in Chapter 7 along with the MADE format. Have some scratch pads printed with the standard MADE format questions and simply fill in the key ideas with a single word or phrase that will jog your memory when dictating:

M: What's the message?
A: So what action next?
      mine—
      reader's—
D: Details—who—
          when—
          where—
          why—
          how—
          how much—

E: Optional evidence enclosed or attached:

Before you dictate, take a moment to fill in the blanks with a word or phrase and then pick up the dictaphone. Following are further guidelines for good, fast dictation:

Practice. Schedule regular dictating times so that you improve your skills.

Gather the information you need before you start writing: copies of correspondence, figures, files. If you have to stop mid-memo or mid-letter to get information, then you have to start over and review the tape to remember where you were.

Talk to an imaginary person. In other words, much like the speaker who picks out a friendly face in the audience to which to direct comments and from whom to get encouragement and nods of appreciation, imagine your reader. Be conversational and address his or her interests in what you have to say.

Decide on the overall layout of the document: sections, headings, etc. This layout will help you in your planning and help the typist in transcribing.

Number, or otherwise identify, your messages. Then, after a long dictating session, when you want to make changes or additions you do not have to spend time explaining to the typist which letter or memo you want to make an insertion into. Identify each document simply by letter, number, or brief subject line.

Don't do things that compete with your voice for your typist's attention. Don't mumble, jumble papers, rattle keys, chew gum, tap the microphone, twirl a pencil, or make any noise that makes the dictation difficult to hear. Otherwise, the finished document may come back to you with blanks and question marks in the margins.

Begin each tape by identifying yourself and the date and type of dictation (correspondence, report on XYZ project, etc.).

Be sure that you help the typist distinguish between text to be typed and instructions to her. I do this by calling my typist by name when the comment is directed to her. Then to return to the text, I say, "back to text now."

Give document information as to whether you're dictating a rough draft or a final copy, what kind of paper to use, and how many copies to whom.

Spell all unfamiliar names, addresses and technical terms.

Give format instructions about placement of column headings, lists (bullets or numbers), line spacing, new paragraphs.

Specify punctuation. Commas particularly are hard to transcribe. The typist doesn't know whether the pause on the tape represents a comma or simply a breath. Additionally, the typist can't tell where parentheses or quotes go until she hears the complete sentence, and then she must go back and make corrections—not difficult to do on a word processor but faster done if the dictator calls out punctuation as he or she goes along. (If thinking about punctuation inhibits your dictating speed, omit it. But have your typist prepare a quick draft and let you correct punctuation if she has a problem with that. You can do several drafts in this method much more quickly than one longhand draft.)

Be sure to give special instructions about print emphasis: "italicize," "bold print," "cap this line," "use numerals for 26 rather than spell out," etc.

Dictate all titles of enclosures or attachments. Not simply, "Put in the enclosures mentioned." Often there's ambiguity about documents you may refer to but do not want included or attached.

Tell the typist where each document ends so she doesn't keep listening to blank tape, thinking there may be more.

If the document is not the routine, give any special instructions for filing.

PUT DESTRUCTION DATES ON YOUR PAPER

On all incoming documents placed in your reading file, you or your secretary should add a destruction date. What's the use in reading a circular informing you of a seminar on May 16, when you find yourself reading the announcement in the middle of June?

Likewise with files. Don't keep things indefinitely. Remember that each four-drawer file costs you about $2,160 annually to maintain. Computer storage is also expensive. An erase date on documents lets your secretary or the word-processing specialists know when they can free the disk space without having to send you a memo listing all titles of your documents and dates of last access. If you wait until months later to decide when to destroy, you'll have to review the files before you give the erase command.

Purge your files at least once every year. Thin files save retrieval time, as well as storage and handling costs.

IGNORE WHAT YOU CAN

Tom Peters and Nancy Austin raise the question: Have you ever seen a top performer fired for his inclination to ignore paperwork? In *A Passion for Excellence*, they cite an incident where the head of Royal Dutch/Shell Malaysia barged into a board meeting unannounced and dumped a suitcase full of forms on the conference table, asking: "Do you want me to fill these out or hunt for oil?" The man eventually became the head of the Shell group.

When you have to choose between getting the real work done and completing the 157 reports the previously mentioned field engineer complained of, spend your time on the more profitable activities and see if the big guys don't leave you alone about the little stuff.

A FINAL NOTE
AND PLAN
OF ACTION

In my writing workshops when I remind participants that commas and periods go inside quote marks, frequently someone will timidly ask, "But how will everybody know this is correct? It looks strange; somebody may think it's wrong." My answer: Yes, they may. But then if they comment, you can set them straight with the whys and wherefores.

Both you and your employees who put these suggestions for cutting paperwork into practice in your own corporate culture may be thinking the same thing: "If I write a margin note instead of a formal, typed memo, will the recipient think I'm lazy?" (No, he'll think you're busy and efficient.) "If I ask my supervisor to give me more details about the audience for my report, won't she think I'm unknowledgeable?" (No, she'll think you aim to please and to prepare a usable report.)

But I do understand the resistance to change that prompts these apprehensions from lower-ranking employees. When we talk about making changes, we usually find physical, psychological, and social resistance: "Will my desk get moved if we take out some of the file cabinets?" "Will I get access to a computer without having to walk across the hall to use one?" "Will my job of processing these forms become obsolete?" "Will the rest of my peers go along with the changes I initiate?" "Will my peers think I'm an uninformed isolate?" "Will my staff think I'm becoming lax in my standards for accuracy?"

All legitimate concerns.

That's why the sweeping changes that this book suggests must be made at the top. Entry-level people usually copy what everybody else is doing. Middle managers model senior managers. It's up to senior managers to implement a plan of action:

1. Use your own staff or an outside ad agency to publicize to employees the paperwork reduction campaign.
2. Make employees aware of how much paperwork costs in terms of writing time, reading time, form-processing time, and record storage and maintenance.
3. Conduct a companywide forms and reports audit or have each department or division conduct its own audits on the paperwork it originates. Insist writers and processors find out what goes where and why.
4. Issue priorities for documents that you consider formal. Assure employees that it's okay to be informal on internal correspondence.
5. Adopt a company format for routine documents so that writers don't waste time reorganizing already-simplified messages.
6. Adopt or write a company style book to eliminate the edit/rewrite/ edit/rewrite syndrome.
7. Investigate the benefits, costs, and break-even point for electronic information and message handling. Consider hiring an information manager.
8. Train employees to write quickly, clearly, and concisely.
9. Reward employees for not generating paperwork. Publicize the names of managers who cure their departments of bureaucratic procedures and forms. Pay bonuses according to savings through less paperwork.

To those senior managers putting these suggestions into action, I repeat once again the axiom, "timing is everything."

When you announce that you will be having someone conduct a forms audit, do it. Don't assign such a project to a committee who may get around to reporting back to you in six months. Best yet, have all areas conduct their own forms audit so they can ferret out the unnecessary and experience the satisfaction of unburdening themselves and their colleagues of the excessive paperwork.

When you announce that internal memos should be handled informally in one of the ways suggested in Chapter 14, so as to save more time for external correspondence to clients and customers, be sure to handle *your* out-going responses informally.

When you announce a company format to follow the MADE guidelines presented in Chapter 7, follow it. Get to the point in your own writing and then quit.

Finally, in implementing these changes, gain others' participation. Let them know who's responsible for what, what benefits will be achieved, how they are to fit into the plan, and how their cooperation will be noted in performance reviews.

Paper has become the panacea for all kinds of problems. Like Scarlett O'Hara, some think, "If we write it down, we can think about it tomorrow." And now paper has become so ingrained into our society that the cure for a mild case of untrustworthiness and forgetfulness has become worse than the disease itself. Paperwork is the disease that threatens to devour our budget and time, demoralize our workers, confuse our customers, reduce our productivity, and stifle our creativity and intrapreneurialism. You now have the diagnosis and the prescription; it's up to you to preach and practice the cure.

BIBLIOGRAPHY

"A Report Should Do More Than Report." *Industry Week*. Vol. 182, No. 8, August 19, 1974, pp. 49-50.

Addams, H. Lon. "Should the Big 8 Teach Communications Skills." *Management Accounting*. Vol. 62, No. 11, May 1981, pp. 37-40.

Andrews, J. Douglas, Norman B. Sigband. "How Effectively Does the 'New' Accountant Communicate? Perceptions By Practitioners and Academics." *Journal of Business Communication*. Vol. 21, No. 2, Spring 1984, pp. 15-24.

"Assessing Management Competency Needs." *Training and Development Journal*. Vol. 34, No. 9, September 1980, pp. 47-51.

Barcomb, David. *Office Automation*. Bedford, Mass.: Digital Press, 1981.

Bates, Gary D. "Upgrading Written Communication—Your Firm's and Your Own." *IEEE Transactions on Professional Communication*. Vol. PC-27, No. 2, June 1984, pp. 89-92.

Bates, Peter. "How to Turn Your Writing into Communications." *Personal Computing*. Vol. 8, No. 10, October 1984, pp. 60-69.

Beam, Henry. "Good Writing: An Underrated Executive Skill." *Human Resource Management*. Vol. 20, No. 1, Spring 1981, pp. 2-7.

"Beefing Up on Electronics Makes Hercules Leaner." *Business Week*, Oct. 8, 1984.

Bentley, Trevor J. *Information, Communication, and the Paperwork Explosion*. New York: McGraw-Hill, 1976, page 26.

Bernstein, Richard E. "Professional Forms Make for Efficient Business." *The Office*. Vol. 95, No. 1, January 1982, page 164.

"Biz Grads' Focus Too Narrow." *USA Today*, May 20, 1985.

Blake, George B. "Ideas for Action: Development, Trends, and Useful Proposals for the Attention of Managers." *Harvard Business Review*. March-April 1978, page 6.

Bly, Robert W. "The Key to a Great Inquiry Fulfillment." *Business Marketing*. Vol. 68, No. 4, April 1983, pp. 92, 95-96.

Booher, Dianna. *The New Secretary*: How to Handle People As Well As You Handle Paper. New York: Facts On File, 1985.

Booher, Dianna. *Send Me a Memo*. New York: Facts On File, Inc., 1984.

Booher, Dianna. *Would You Put That in Writing?* New York: Facts On File, Inc., 1983.

Branham, James E. "Getting Through the Day: How CEO's Manage...Whatever It Is They Do." *Industry Week*. Vol. 220, No. 3, February 6, 1984, pp. 36-42.

Brillhart, L. V., M. B. Debs. "A Survey of Technical Writing Courses in Engineering Colleges." *Engineering Education*, November 1983, pp. 110-113.

Broughton, Bradford B. "A Key Course to Unlock Communication: Letter Writing." *IEEE Transactions on Professional Communication*. Vol. PC-27, No. 4, December 1984, pp. 193-196.

Budd, John F., Jr. "Is the Focus of Communication on Target?" *Sloan Management Review*. Vol. 24, No. 1, Fall 1982, pp. 51-53.

Burgess, John H. *Human Factors in Forms Design*. Chicago: Nelson-Hall Press, 1984.

Burgess, Priscilla. "The Tyranny of Words." *Computer World*. April 16, 1984, ID Section, pp. 1-10.

"Business Awakes to the Crisis in Education." *Business Week*. July 4, 1983, page 32.

Buyers, Robert. "Documentation of Business Procedures—A New Technique for an Old Problem." *Journal of Systems Management*. Vol. 35, No. 10, October 1984, pp. 16-19.

Cardinelli, Frank S. "The Specialized Skill in Designing Business Forms." *The Office*. Vol. 95, No. 1, January 1982, page 141.

Casari, Laura E. "Required: Three Hours in Technical Communications—Paradigm for a Paradox." *IEEE Transactions on Professional Communications*. Vol. PC-27, No. 3, September 1984, pp. 116.

Crook, Stan, Mark Crawford. "Pressing for a 'Paperless' Government." *Business Week*. March 25, 1985, pp. 29-30.

David, Carol, Donna Stine. "Measuring Skills Games and Attitudes of Adult Writers in Short Courses." *American Business Communication Association* (ABCA Bulletin). March 1984, pp. 14-20.

Davis, Richard. "Technical Writing in Industry and Government." *Journal of Technical Writing Communications.* Vol. 7, 1977, pp. 235-252.

Davis, Stanley M. *Managing Corporate Culture.* Cambridge, Mass.: Ballinger Publishing Company, 1984.

Deal, Terrence E., Allan A. Kennedy. *Corporate Cultures: The Rites and Rituals of Corporate Life.* Reading Mass.: Addison-Wesley Publishing Company, Inc., 1982.

DeLong, David. "Toss Out Useless Paperwork." *Inc.* June 1981, pp. 70, 72.

Denton, D. Keith. "Protecting against Communication (Fallout)." *Management World.* Vol. 12, No. 3, April 1983, pp. 28.

"Determine How Best to Use Time." *Rough Notes.* Vol. 126, No. 9, September 1983, page 26.

Distribution for Traffic and Transportation Decision Makers. Vol. 84, No. 2, February 1985, page 70.

Dreilinger, Craig. "Paperwork Style and Managerial Effectiveness." *Management Review.* Vol. 69, No. 1, January 1980, pp. 21-24.

Fielden, John S., Ronald E. Duelek. "How to Use Bottom-line Writing in Corporate Communications." *Business Horizons.* Vol. 27, No. 4, July-August 1984, pp. 24.

"Filing: Cheaper by the Billion." *Modern Office Technology.* Vol. 30, No. 2, February 1985, pp. 70-72.

Flatley, Marie E. "A Comparative Analysis of the Written Communication of Managers at Various Organizational Levels in the Private Business Sector." *Journal of Business Communication.* Vol. 19, No. 3, Summer 1982, pp. 35-49.

Foegen, J. H. "Let's Develop Employee Assistance Programs to Teach Reading and Writing." *Personnel Journal.* Vol. 63, No. 3, March 1984, pp. 83-85.

Friedman, Stan. "Agents Look to Outwrite Competition." *National Underwriter.* Life and Health Insurance Edition, March 9, 1985, pp. 4.

Gilsdorf, J. W. "Slaying the Paper Dragon." *Supervisory Management.* Vol. 28, No. 4, April 1983, pp. 2-11.

Gorman, Kenneth L. "Improving Dictation Skills: A Checklist for Procedure." *Office.* Vol. 96, No. 5, November 1982, pp. 179-180.

Grossman, Lee. "A Manager's Approach to the Paperwork Explosion." *Management Review.* September 1978, pp. 57-61.

Grossman, Lee. *Fat Paper...Diets for Trimming Paperwork.* New York: McGraw-Hill, 1976, page 84.

"Growing Bank Credits Microfilm for Easing its Paperwork Problem." *The Office.* Vol. 94, No. 3, September 1981, pp. 122-124.

Hackos, Joann T. "Teaching Problem-Solving Strategies in the Technical Communication Classroom." *IEEE Transactions on Professional Communication.* Vol. PC-27, No. 4, December 1984, pp. 180-184.

Haskell, Debra L. "White Collar Productivity: Management's No. 1 Concern." *Modern Office Procedures,* September 1979, page 46.

Hayes, James L. "Putting It in Writing: A Critical Executive Skill." *Credit and Financial Management.* Vol. 85, No. 4, April 1983, pp. 27, 45.

Henning, Jo-el. "The Necessity of Support Systems." *Training & Development Journal.* June 1985, page 14.

"Hide This Article from Your Staff." *Training and Development Journal.* July 1985, page 10.

Hilchey, Robert E. "World of a White Collar: People, Paper, and Productivity." *Journal of Methods-Time Measurement.* Vol. 9, No. 4, 1982, pp. 16-19.

Hill, James W. "The Practical Application of Completed Staff Work." *Supervisory Management.* Vol. 25, No. 6, June 1980, pp. 37.

Hirt, John L. "Besting the Paperwork Beast of Burden." *Journal of Forms Management.* Vol. 9, No. 2, July/December 1984, pp. 6-7.

Horn, William Dennis. "Computer-Assisted Writing Instruction at Clarkson University." *IEEE Transactions on Professional Communication.* Vol. PC-27, No. 4, December 1984, pp. 197-200.

Horton, Forest, Jr. "IRM: The Invisible Resolution." *Computer World.* Vol. 16, No. 33, August 16, 1982, pp. 108 (in depth).

Iacocca, Lee, William Novak. *Iacocca: An Autobiography.* New York: Bantam, 1984.

"IBM, Brazil, Helps Tame a Bureaucratic Brontosaurus." *International Management.* Vol. 39, No. 11, November 1984, pp. 82.

"Information Management System Hems Firm's Paperwork." *Computer World.* Vol. 18, No. 13, March 26, 1984, pp. 43-45.

Kalthoff, Robert J., Col. Leonard S. Lee. *Productivity and Records Automation.* Englewood Cliffs, N.J.: Prentice-Hall, Inc., 1981.

Kimel, William R., Melford E. Monsees. "Engineering Graduates: How Good Are They?" *Engineering Education.* Vol. 70, November 1979, pp. 210-212.

Kleinschrod, Walter. "They've Been to College, But They Still Can't Write." *Administrative Management*. September 1977, page 27.

Knapp, Joan. "Can Engineers Write?" *IEEE Transactions on Professional Communication*. Vol. PC-27, No. 1, March 1984, pp. 10-13.

Knox, Frank M. *Managing Paperwork: A Key to Productivity*. New York: Thomond Press, 1980.

Kuttner, Monroe S. *Managing the Paperwork Pipeline*. New York: John Wiley & Sons, 1978.

Lamont-Brown, Raymond. "The Small Businessman and the Financial Paperwork Bogey." *Accountancy*. Vol. 91, No. 1041, May 1980, page 167.

Leaf, R. Benton. "Electronic Mail, Automated Microfilm Retrieval Speed Recovery of Truncated Checks for Baltimore Banks." *Journal of Information and Image Management*. December 1984, pp. 45-47.

LeBoeuf, Michael. "Melting the Paper Blizzard." *Marketing Times*. Vol. 30, No. 1, January-February 1983, pp. 5-6.

Lee, Chris. "Training at Loews Corp: If It's Not Broken... " *Training*. April 1985, pp. 43-45.

Lee, Col. Leonard S. "Information Management at the Crossroads." *Records Management Quarterly*. Vol. 16, No. 2, April 1982, pp. 5.

Leipzig, John S., Elizabeth More. "Organizational Communication: A Review and Analysis of Three Current Approaches to the Field." *Journal of Business Communication*. Vol. 19, No. 4, Fall 1982, pp. 77-92.

LeVan, Gary D. "Forms Redesign Cuts Bank's Paperwork." *Journal of Systems Management*. Vol. 31, No. 2, February 1980, pp. 38-39.

Levanthal, Naomi. "Making the Most of Writing Assignments." *Supervisory Management*. Vol. 27, No. 9, September 1982, pp. 16-19.

Levine, Edward L. "Let's Talk: Tools for Spotting and Correcting Communication Problems." *Supervisory Management*. Vol. 25, No. 7, July 1980, pp. 25-37.

Levine, Edward L. "Let's Talk: Understanding One-to-One Communication." *Supervisory Management*. Vol. 25, No. 5, May 1980, pp. 6-12.

Livingston, Dennis. "Teleconferencing." *Computer World*. Vol. 16, No. 48A, December 1982, pp. 65-67.

Lowe, John R. "When You Report, Really Report." *National Underwriter (Property/Casualty)*. Vol. 87, No. 22, June 3, 1983, pp. 19, 33.

Ludlow, Michael P. "Voice Messaging: Taking A Run At Cost Justification." *On Communications*. Vol. 1, No. 1, November 1984, pp. 40-44.

Lyman, Guy C. III. "Voice Messaging Comes of Age." *Speech Technology*. Aug.—Sept. 1984.

Mackenzie, Alec R. "Sound Time Management Can Make a Difference." *National Underwriter*. Life and Health Insurance Edition, September 12, 1984, p. 4.

Max, Robert R. *Training and Development Journal*. Vol. 39, No. 3, March 1985, pp. 50-51.

McKean, Kevin S. "Computers Right Writers' Wrongs." *International Management*. Vol. 37, No. 5, May 1982, pp. 19-20.

Mescon, Timothy S., George S. Vocikis. "Federal Regulation—What are the Costs?" *Business*. Vol. 32, No. 1, January/March 1982, pp. 33-39.

Miller, Phyllis A. Ph. D. "Reading Demands in a High-Technology Industry." *Journal of Reading*. November 1982, pp. 109-115.

Moran, Alfred J., Jr. "Fighting the Paper War—And Winning." *Financial Executive*. Vol. 50, No. 9, September 1982, pp. 52-56.

Moran, Alfred J., Jr. "Fighting the Paper War with Business Forms Efficiency." *The Office*. Vol. 96, No. 3, September 1982, pp. 80.

Mundale, Susan. "Why More CEO's are Mandating Listening and Writing Training." *Training Magazine*. October 1980, pp. 37.

Nygren, William V. *Business Forms Management*. New York: Amacom, 1980.

Olivis, Lewis, Tom Innman. "What Concerns Today's Trainers." *Training and Development Journal*. Vol. 37, No. 7, July 1983, pp. 62.

Paul, Jerry. "Salinas Trims Paperwork Thanks to Data Communications Network." *Data Management*. Vol. 23, No. 3, March 1985, pp. 54-57.

Peacock, William E. *Corporate Combat*. New York: Facts On File, 1984, page 122.

Peters, Thomas J., Nancy K. Austin. *A Passion for Excellence*. New York: Random House, 1985.

Peters, Thomas J., Robert H. Waterman, Jr. *In Search of Excellence*. New York: Harper & Row, 1982.

Pinsker, Sanford. "Managing the Writing Process." *Business*. Vol. 33, No. 4, October/December 1983, pp. 47-48.

Place, Irene, David J. Hyslop. *Records Management: Controlling Business Information*. Reston, Va.: Reston Publishing Company, 1982.

Poppel, Harvey L. "Who Needs the Office of the Future?" *Harvard Business Review*. No. 82610, November-December 1982.

"Project ELF: The Twenty-five Percent Solution to Business Expenses!" *Journal of Micrographics*. December 1982, pp. 18-22.

Quick, Thomas L. *Person to Person Managing*. New York: St. Martin, 1977.

Rader, Martha H., Ph.D. "Suffering from Information Overload?" *Management World*. Vol. 8, No. 11, December 1979, pp. 7-10.

Rayner, Derek G. "A Battle Won and the War on Paper Bureaucracy." *Harvard Business Review*. January-February 1975, pp. 8.

Reep, Dianna C. "Stop Writing the Wrongs." *Personnel Journal*. Vol. 63, No. 9, September 1984, pp. 68-72.

Russell, W. James. "Good Forms Management Improves Productivity." *The Office*. Vol. 99, No. 5, May 1984, pp. 8-84.

Savage, William G. "Sharpening Your Communications." *Management World*. Vol. 11, No. 8, August 1982, pp. 26-27, 31.

Sharplin, Arthur, Wanda Sharplin. "Manager, Faculty, and Student Attitudes about Communication Skills." *Northeast Louisiana Business Review*. Fall/Winter 1983, pp. 13, 15-16.

Sloan, Alfred P., Jr. *My Years With General Motors*. Garden City, N. Y.: Doubleday & Company, Inc., 1964.

Southern, Arlen D. "The CEO as Chief Financial Communicator." *Directors and Boards*. Vol. 9, No. 1, Fall 1984, pp. 24.

Stein, Judith, Marya Holcomb. "Helping Someone Else Write More Effectively." *Supervisory Management*. Vol. 25, No. 11, November 1980, pp. 2-9.

Strassman, Paul. "Information Payoff." *Computer World*. Vol. 19, No. 6, February 11, 1985, pp. 15-32 (in depth).

"Survey Sinks Myths about Office Automation Revolution." *Training and Development Journal*. July 1985, pp. 14-15.

Sutcliffe, J. Raymond. "A Major Opportunity for Office Cost Reduction." *The Office*. Vol. 93, No. 4, April 1981, pp. 79-81.

"System Bails Out Troopers from Paperwork." *Computer World*. Vol. 17, No. 45, November 7, 1983, page 43.

"The Automated Office: Waging a Paper War." *ICP Insurance Software*. Vol. 9, No. 1, Spring 1984, page 8.

"The Truncation Debate: Should Business Bother with the Paper Mountain?" *Savings & Loan News*. United States League of Savings Associations. Vol. 101, No. 7, July 1980, pp. 38-42.

Timmons, J. "Increasing the Efficiency of Office Workers as a Means to Halt Inflation." *The Office*. July 1979, pp. 124-125.

Treese, Lorett Ortalli. "Getting Organized for Good Communication." *Supervision*. Vol. 45, No. 2, February 1983, pp. 9-10, 20.

Tuttle, Thomas C., D. Scott Sink. "Taking the Threat Out of Productivity Measurement." *National Productivity Review*. Vol. 4, No. 1, Winter 1984, pp. 24-32.

"Voice Mail Is Corning's Link with World-Wide Operations." *The Office Magazine*. August 1984.

Wahlen, Tim. "Developing an Inhouse Business and Technical Writing Course." *IEEE Transactions On Professional Communication*. Vol. PC-26, No. 4, December 1983, pp. 160-161.

"Westinghouse Stops 'Telephone Tag' with Store-and-Forward Voice Messaging." *Communications News*. May 1982.

"What Undid Jarmin: Paperwork Paralysis." *Business Week*. January 24, 1977, pp. 67-68.

Wikoff, Charles. "Report Prepared Via WP Put Smile on Realtor's Face." *Computer World*. Vol. 15, No. 36, September 7, 1981, pp. 67-68.

Woodall, Robert C. "Managing Information as a Resource." *Records Management Quarterly*. Vol. XIV, No. 3, July 1980, pp. 5-8.

Woolsey, Gene. "Corporate Style, Corporate Substance, and the Sting." *IEEE Transactions on Professional Communication*. Vol. PC-23, No. 2, June 1980, pp. 67-69.

Work, Clemens P. "Washington's Red Tape Just Keeps Rolling Out." *U.S. News and World Report*. Vol. 94, No. 13, April 4, 1983, page 62.

Wright, Patrica, Fraser Reid. "Written Information: Some Alternatives to Prose for Expressing the Outcome of Complex Contingencies." *Journal of Applied Psychology*. Vol. 57, No. 2, 1973, pp. 160-166.

INDEX